KENILWORTH:

The Story of the ABBEY

by

Harry Sunley & Norman Stevens

The Pleasaunce Press

1995

First Published by The Pleasaunce Press
at 32^B, Wilton Place,
London, SW1X 8SH
1995

ISBN   0 90237208 4 Boards
        0 90237209 2 Papercover

British Library Cataloguing in Publication Data.
A catalogue record for this book is available from the British Library.

Harry Sunley, BSc (Hons), is a Chartered Engineer who spent most of his working life
on rocketry. Since 1962 he has taken an intense interest in local history.

Norman Stevens, BA, DipTh, studied theology at Durham University and has been associated
with Kenilworth for over thirty years. He taught for some years at the former
Grammar School and founded both the bookshop now in Talisman Square,
and the Pleasaunce Press, which has published several local history books.

The Publishers would like to thank Mrs Eileen Tisdale and the Kenilworth
Weekly News for the use of the photograph shown as Fig 14b,
and Mr John Ellam for his cover design.

Printed and bound in Great Britain at The University of Warwick

CONTENTS

CHAPTERS

FIGURES

PREFACE

This may be the finished book,
but it is not the end of the story

St Benedict

There is a need for a book on Kenilworth Abbey and its canons. Unlike Kenilworth Castle, the Abbey has been neglected: apart from the buildings themselves, past accounts have consisted largely of isolated snippets from Dugdale and various charters, repeated parrot fashion by the Victoria County History and others.

It has been our aim to produce a systematic account, interpreting the historical events so that the lay reader may understand something of what was happening in the Abbey Fields from the 12th to the 16th centuries. In the process, we have found some hitherto unrecognised facets.

The buildings of the Abbey are not dealt with in any depth. E Carey-Hill's report on the 1922/3 excavation[4] is the most detailed work available, although further study is merited.

On the spiritual side, it has not been easy to get 'close' to the canons. Their writings are few, and hence we have had to extrapolate. Conventions and beliefs have changed radically even within our own lifetime; thus in studying the canons, we are not looking at a single frame, but a number of frames spanning more than 400 years. Therefore, for instance, because silence may not have been strictly observed at one point in time, it does not follow that it was never strictly observed.

This is an account of the canons who breathed our air, lived, prayed, worked and died in Kenilworth, leaving little enough memorial. This is the most in-depth study so far attempted, but it is not claimed to be the ultimate definitive work. Furthermore, we will not be dismayed if evidence conflicting with our interpretations comes to light. History is, after all, like a living organism that has, constantly, to shed its 'dead' cells. We have only to consider St Benedict's remark above.

Finally, this is not so much the result of poring over ancient manuscripts by candle-light, but research at many libraries and record offices, absorbing every word that could be found on Mediæval Kenilworth and the people associated with it.

Harry Sunley   August 1995   Norman Stevens

ACKNOWLEDGEMENTS

There are too many people and organisations to thank individually; a list of references is given at the back, and we thank all those who have toiled in the past to give us invaluable background. We dedicate this work, however, to our patient wives.

INTRODUCTION

But history, real solemn history, I cannot be interested in.....
It is very tiresome; and yet I often think that it is odd
that it should be so dull, for a great deal of it must be invention.

Catherine Morland in *Northanger Abbey*
Jane Austen, 1803

A short distance to the east of the famous and imposing Kenilworth Castle lay the Abbey of St Mary, an equally imposing complex of buildings on the south-facing slope of the valley of Finham Brook. Its line of fishponds and millpools extended from the great Castle Mere, right through to what is now School Lane Meadow.

Founded *c* 1122 by Geoffrey de Clinton, Chamberlain and Treasurer to Henry I, the Augustinian Priory of St Mary was, at its peak, a community of some 70 to 100 souls working in the service of God. It was the first of the six Augustinian houses in Warwickshire, the Augustinians having more houses here, and in fact in England, than any other order. Its income from its extensive properties was the second highest of any house in Warwickshire and was in the top 10% of all Augustinian houses. Unusually for an Augustinian house, it was the mother house to three cells, Brooke, Calwich and Stone; and, also unusually, it came under royal patronage by the early thirteenth century. At about 1447 it was raised to the status of abbey, an honour bestowed on only nine other Augustinian houses. It fell at the Dissolution in 1538 and now there remains all too little of a once important establishment.

The only 'in house' documents that have survived are a series of early charters relating to the canons' possessions, known as the 'Harley 3650' and the 'ADD 47677', both in the British Library. They have been translated by Watson[44], but not yet published. Any other documents that survived the Dissolution may have been lost in a fire in the chambers of James West, solicitor, in 1736 when only the Harley 3650 was saved, and a fire at Birmingham Library in 1879. Thus great use has been made of the various external documents which make reference to Kenilworth; these include Domestic State Papers, Papal Registers and Letters, Fine Rolls, Liberate Rolls, *Regesta Regum Normanorum* &c, &c. A largely untapped source remains, the Registers of the Bishops of Coventry & Lichfield. Many of these exist only in their Latin manuscript form and, being available on micro-film, offer a challenge to a future researcher.

In the following chapters, the origin of the Augustinian canons, and the other half of the equation, the origins of Kenilworth, will be explored. A picture will then be built up of the Priory/Abbey and its inmates, looking over the shoulder at times to see what was happening elsewhere.

SOME TERMS EXPLAINED

The word 'Austin', a diminutive of 'Augustinian', is frequently used; the earliest recorded use was by Wycliffe in 1384, and Chaucer refers to St Augustine as *Austyn*. Despite the use of 'Austin' by that great writer on the subject, the Revd John C Dickinson [12], we will use 'Augustinian'. 'Austen' is another variation, and an Augustinian can also be an 'Austiner'. The canons were also commonly known as the 'Black Canons' because of their garb. Austin Friars are quite separate, and are dealt with in the Appendix.

The earliest canons were clerics with a pastoral rôle, forming the chapter of a cathedral, the seat of a bishop. They were (and still are) *secular canons*, not living in accordance with the *regulae,* or rules, of an Order. The Augustinian canons, on the other hand, were *Canons Regular*, priests living the common life, exactly as monks did, but under the Rule of St Augustine, rather than of St Benedict.

In the following, the terms 'Priory' and 'Abbey' will both be used depending on the actual status of the house at the time referred to. For most orders, a monastery attached to a cathedral was a priory, run by a prior, the bishop being in effect the abbot. An independent house was usually an abbey. A case in point is Coventry which was founded as an abbey, but when the bishop moved his seat there, it was reduced to a priory. A Benedictine priory was usually a house that came under the jurisdiction of an abbey. The Augustinians, however, did not follow this pattern; almost all their houses were founded as priories – reflecting their distant cathedral origins – only a few being founded as, or becoming, abbeys. An abbot had a rather higher status than a prior, and some had the right of summons to Parliament; the Abbots of the Augustinian houses at Bristol, Cirencester, Osney and Waltham were also licensed by the Pope to wear bishops' mitres.

The term *religious* covers any person who has taken the three religious vows of poverty, chastity and obedience, and generally excludes parish priests and bishops, though not in every case. A *monk* is a man who has taken vows and who lives in a *monastery* but is not necessarily an ordained priest. A *nun* is a female monk (but who could not be ordained a priest) living in a *nunnery*. A *convent* is a company of women or men living in the discipline of an order and under a superior; thus monks, nuns and canons form convents. Kenilworth is referred to in charters as the 'Prior and Convent of Kenilworth'. The words 'house' and 'monastery' can be used also to describe

the establishments where all types of 'religious' live, i.e. monks, nuns, canons, etc.

There are terminological traps that may catch the unwary, such as the word 'rectory' which is not only where a rector lives, but is principally a form of tithe, as is also a 'vicarage'. Likewise, a 'farm' is not only where old McDonald keeps his pigs, but is primarily a lease. A pension is not just what is received on retirement, but any annual payment. Terms like these will, as far as possible, be explained as they occur.

There are associated topics that do not form a part of the main stream, and having relevance, they are included in the Appendices, the attention of the reader being directed to them where appropriate.

In order to put flesh on the bones, a 'Who's Who' of the inmates of the house has been included as the final chapter. From these small beginnings, it may be possible to build up a wider biography of some of these people.

The decision has been taken to annotate only major references in the text; too numerous references can be an irritant. However, in establishing the facts on which the book is based, an informal work, 'Material for the Augustinian Canons of Kenilworth', was prepared. This is structured chronologically only, but gives the sources of all entries. A copy of this will be lodged in the Warwick Records Office and Kenilworth Library.

I DEVELOPMENT OF THE ORDER

We urge you who form a religious community
to put the following precepts into practice.

The start of the Rule of St Augustine

It is, perhaps, difficult in this relatively materialistic age to understand the motives of people who were prepared to renounce all possessions and live an enclosed life that, by our standards, would have been both hard and monotonous. Was it for the salvation of their souls, or was the life in a convent preferable to the hard life outside? Or were there higher motives? Monasticism was not created overnight, but the result of what we would call today a 'lengthy development process'.

Before Christianity became tolerated under the Edict of Milan in 313, most Christians lived a life of renunciation, prayer and service; the second coming of the Lord was imminent, and preparation for divine judgement was a priority. The politicisation of Christianity by Constantine had reduced this urgency for all but the fervent minority, who continued to seek their salvation in the austere life; and it was they who fled to the deserts of Egypt, Syria and Palestine. There, two distinct modes of life were adopted; the solitary life of the desert hermit (*eremos,* Gk, a desert) where the search for God was individual, the most famous exponent of which was perhaps St Simeon Stylites. The other was cenobitical (*koinos,* Gk, common), living in communities, brought into some form of order by people such as St Anthony (originally a hermit) and St Basil. This movement travelled west and the beginning of the 6th century saw the emergence of St Benedict with his rule for monks that was to be the backbone of mediæval monasticism.

THE CANONS

From the 4th century, all priests living in a clergy house, and directly responsible to the bishop, were referred to as *canonici* (because they appeared in an official list, a *canon*), and they became the *ordo canonicus.* They were distinct from private chaplains, monks and nuns who were not servants of the local church. The way of life of these canons varied from the severe, 'Augustinian' type, to the more relaxed where the canons could 'live out' and were 'devoted to wives and secular pursuits'. Whilst mandatory in the cloister, attempts to force celibacy on priests were far from universally successful, and it was not until the Lateran Councils of 1123 and 1139 that the marriage of priests was finally declared invalid and sinful.

Boniface, born in Crediton *c* 680, was one of the great reformers of the Northern church, presiding over two important synods, where he championed the cause for creating common households for cathedral clergy. At the Council of Aachen in 816-7, the *canons* or rules for establishments of priests, were evolved, based largely on Benedictine monasticism. This reform appeared popular for a while, but Europe, including Britain, suffered invasions and disorders which attenuated the good work that had been done. Stability was restored by the tenth century. The towns began to grow again and several clergy served different areas of them. However, the life of the unmarried parish priest can be very lonely, and enthusiasm can wane easily, as we know only too well even today. The priests of a town began to club together, as it were, for mutual support – the nearest equivalent today is the 'team ministry', comprising perhaps, in the Church of England, members of, say, the Company of Mission Priests – to pray and say the offices together, to share servants, meals and so on. Each group, or, literally, house, kept its house rules, and, as the church was strictly hierarchical and closely governed, the local bishop had to ratify any arrangement.

Sometimes the grouping focused on a cathedral, but not necessarily. The cathedral foundations of this sort tended to remain unchanged in regulation and ethos; and most of the non-monastic cathedrals of England at the time of the Conquest were of this looser secular pattern. But changes to the others were soon to come.

Meanwhile, in the 4th century, St Augustine of Hippo emerged in North Africa (he is not to be confused with the Augustine who came in 597 to convert the English and become the first archbishop of Canterbury). His Rule was based on precepts he devised for his sister, a superior of a house of 'discordant' nuns. Details of his life, and an abbreviated form of his Rule are given in the Appendix. The Rule was to remain latent, however, for a few centuries.

During the great European monastic revival of the 11th century, a house of canons was founded in 1039 at St Ruf, near Avignon; so far lacking a rule, St Augustine's was 'rediscovered' and adapted. Lawrence [25] says that this was one of the great discoveries of the 11th century – *like America, it had been there all the time, and, although it was not precisely what was being looked for, the world was never quite the same afterwards.* The Lateran

Councils of 1059 and 1063 recognised and blessed all those clergy who wished to embrace the full common or 'Apostolic' life, and the order, as Dickinson [12] put it, received its 'birth certificate'. From this, the foundation of a number of houses in France followed.

TO ENGLAND

One movement of canons that started in Lorraine spread to England when King Harold founded the church of Holy Cross at Waltham in 1061; it was served by seven canons and a provost. However, no particular rule was adopted at that time, although it later became Augustinian, and further such houses were set up at Canterbury (c 1081) and Huntingdon (1086-91).

The only universal rule that had been adopted in England up to that time was that of St Benedict. The opportunity of introducing a new order was seized upon, both for its novelty, and for certain attractive features. The name of Augustine was prestigious; the Rule allowed considerable latitude, although it was seen to resemble the mode of life of the apostles more closely than the Benedictine rule. Another important factor was that an Augustinian house could be founded for rather less money than a Benedictine house which required a certain opulence from the start. Southern [32] quotes an income of £3 a year to support an Augustinian canon, against at least three times that amount for a Benedictine monk. A great spiritual benefit was to be gained from founding a monastic house, and the ability to do this at lower cost brought many benefactors into the 'house-founding' class. This is why there were to be approximately twice as many Augustinian houses in England as Benedictine, although, of course, there were other orders of monks and canons to come.

The first Augustinian house in England is generally considered to have been founded at Colchester in 1104-6; Dunmow (Essex) followed immediately, and then St Mary Overy, which is today Southwark Cathedral, both founded by leading barons – 'New Men'. Next came Henry's Queen, Matilda's, foundation of the first monastery within London Wall, Holy Trinity, Aldgate in c 1108. During the rest of Henry's reign, the order expanded rapidly, as indeed did all existing and new Orders during the 12th century. During the reign of Henry I (1100-1135), several Augustinian houses were founded by members of the Royal Court, including, of course, Geoffrey de Clinton, founder of Kenilworth.

Figure 1 is a histogram of the foundation dates for a number of Augustinian houses where it is seen that Kenilworth was one of the earlier houses. There had been some 251 houses by the time of the Dissolution, including temporary sites and houses that changed order. The Order was well established in England, particularly on the east side of the country but only a few houses in West Wales and one in Scotland. The relatively high concentration in the east was to be found in East Anglia in particular.

A CHANGE OF ROLE

England was well behind the Continent in Church reform in the early 12th century: and it certainly did need reform. When finally the Augustinian rule came over, it was first adopted in populous towns — Colchester, Southwark, London and Huntingdon — but without cathedral connection, and filled a pastoral need. This followed the earlier pattern of France and Germany. But houses were also founded in much more remote parts: Dunmow, Ivychurch, Llanthony, Hexham, Bridlington, prefiguring the later austere but popular Cistercian movement. This is a clear indication that the priests, gathering themselves under the Augustinian umbrella in these remote places, were more interested in monasticism than pastoralia.

So, given the lower cost of Augustinian houses, a land owner would have reckoned that the canons' prayers for his and his family's souls were every bit as effective as the monks', if not more so, as the former were able to say masses individually for them; monks generally at that time were not. Hence the non-urban foundations tended to be on or near the founder's 'honour' or home locality, and smaller than the Benedictine houses.

It is interesting to note that, although Henry I was involved in founding several Augustinian houses, when it came to founding his own Mausoleum it was the great Benedictine-Cluniac house of Reading that came into existence, on which he spent far more than on any other monastic project. The Augustinians were pursuing modes of monasticism that were wholly incompatible with a huge Royal Chantry spending its life in elaborate music and ritual for the benefit of a king's soul.

After this period of indecision, the Augustinians moved increasingly away from pastoral activities. M Deansley [11] comments: *Superiors found it undesirable that canons should leave the dormitory in the middle of the night to take the sacraments to the sick, and the service of a small outlying cell was found similarly to unfit a canon for the stricter regular life.*

The essential difference between monks and canons was now really the matter of priesthood. It was only later that monks tended to be ordained priests and say masses regularly. Otherwise they both lived under a similar regimen.

STATUS

The order achieved some eminence in England, although perhaps not as much as on the Continent. Nicholas Breakespeare, born near St Albans, is thought to have had early contact with the Augustinians at Merton Priory, Surrey: he went on to become Abbot at St Ruf, and then the only English-born Pope, Adrian IV, 1154-9. William Corbeil, the first Prior of St Osyth, became archbishop of Canterbury 1123-39. A number of bishops identified themselves with the order, including Anselm, archbishop of Canterbury 1093-1114. Thomas Becket was educated at Merton, where Prior Robert became his friend. Dickinson suggests that on his election to the see of Canterbury, he returned to Merton where he took the habit of a regular canon. A number of scholars graced the order, and the Oxford house of St Frideswide was connected with the foundation of the University.

The Augustinians in England were characterised by their independence of continental influence, unlike the Benedictines. Few were started as foreign colonies. This led to flexibility and the ensuing individualism of houses that became a popular feature of the order. Guidance was obtained primarily from the bishop and, later, the three-yearly chapter of the Order. There were, however, the so-called independent congregations or colonies of Augustinians, such as the house founded at Jerusalem in 1114, which formed colonies, of which St Sepulchre, Warwick was one. Another group, the Præmonstratensians based on Prémontre in France, had houses in England, and the group based on St Victor in Paris included St Augustine, Bristol, now Bristol Cathedral. The other main group, the Arrouaisians, also French, had houses in England, including Arbury in Warwickshire.

The order waxed until the middle of the 13th century, but, by the 15th century, was waning. Cardinal Wolsey was one its champions, urging the order to build a college at Oxford. It was happenstance that he died at the Augustinian Abbey of Leicester, 29 November, 1530, on his way to London to face a charge of high treason. The order in England and Wales became defunct at the Dissolution, but continued, in France, for instance, up to the Revolution. Today's French and English houses have been refounded since those bleak days.

FOUNDATION DATES OF AUGUSTINIAN HOUSES IN ENGLAND

1100	+++++ +++++ +	*c* 1105 Colchester
1120	+++++ +++++ +++++ +++++ +++++ +++++ +++	*c* 1122 Kenilworth
1140	+++++ +++++ +++++ +++++	
1160	+++++ +++++ +++++ +++++ +++++ +	
1180	+++++ +++++ +++++ +++	
1200	+++++ +++++	
1220	+++++ +	
1240	+++	
1260	++++	
1280	+	
1300	+	
1320	+++	
1340	++	
1360		
1380		

Data from Dickinson [12]

FIG. 1

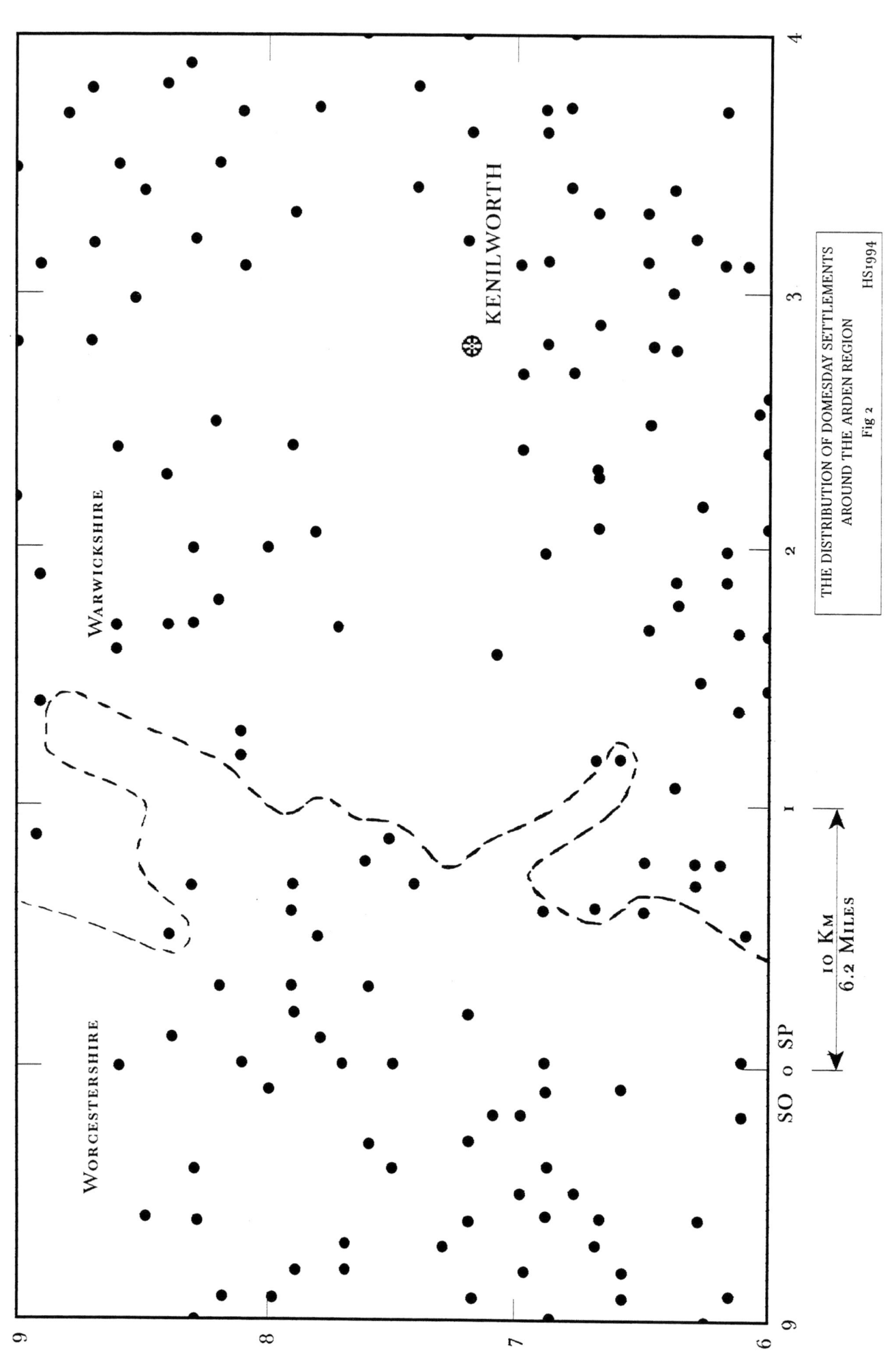

THE DISTRIBUTION OF DOMESDAY SETTLEMENTS
AROUND THE ARDEN REGION   HS1994

Fig 2

KENILWORTH

WARWICKSHIRE

WORCESTERSHIRE

10 KM
6.2 MILES

SO o SP

II THE CANONS & KENILWORTH

*In Chinewrde Richard the Forester holds
3 virgates of land from the King...*

Start of the Domesday Entry for Kenilworth

The first mention of the township we know today as Kenilworth appears in the Domesday Book of 1086 as a part of William I's manor of Stoneleigh. Dugdale [14] confuses the issue by suggesting that another Domesday community, *Optone*, was the High Street area of Kenilworth. This is now discounted for several reasons, not least of which is that the Castle and Priory would have been of Optone, instead of Kenilworth. Optone can be identified with Leek Wootton, which was known as *Vttone* by the 12th Century.

The Domesday community of Kenilworth was small by any local standards, having an area under cultivation of 3 virgates, estimated as 90 acres, compared with an average community size of 620 acres for Warwickshire. There does not appear to have been a church; Warwickshire Domesday does not mention churches as such (unlike, for instance the Domesday for Kent), but note is made of where there are priests, for example, two for Stoneleigh, but none for Kenilworth. Only 49 of the 245 communities in Warwickshire were recorded as having priests.

An important aspect of Kenilworth to be learnt from Domesday is that, whilst there were numerous communities to the south and east, there is a sector from the north backing round to the west, where communities are sparse, as seen in Figure 2. The population in this area is less than a third of that in the south of the county. As P A Nicklin [27] put it, there is an absence of Domesday manors between Coventry and Alvechurch, and that the infertile nature of the land has resulted in a number of place-names including the word 'heath'. Thus Domesday Kenilworth was on the south-east edge of an undeveloped area, the remnants of the so-called Forest of Arden.

It was in this small and unimportant community that Henry I granted Geoffrey de Clinton land for the Priory, his Castle, park and fishponds and for his borough. But why?

Apart from the usual reasons quoted – the protection of communications, &c – Henry I was concerned at the possibility of a military threat from the de Montforts at Beaudesert Castle, on the southern edge of the Arden; this is discussed in detail by Stevens [33]. With the need for a castle to control the situation, Henry had to choose a site, and a source of suitable building stone was an important factor.

Just to the west of Kenilworth there is a north-south geographical fault, which, in effect, brought sandstone to the surface at Kenilworth, but not to the west of it. Thus Kenilworth became one of the most westerly sites where quarrying could take place; Little Virginia, just to the east of the Castle later became a quarry site as well as a masons' yard, and there were quarries at the back of High Street, and in Priorsfield, just to the north of the Castle. Thus Kenilworth was a logical place for a castle, which, sited at the end of the convergent valley, was ideal for creating a dam and water defences. It was also Henry I's demesne or own land.

Its site decided, Stevens has indicated that work proceeded on the Castle apace in the first half of the 12th century. This is at variance with the expressed views of some authorities (for example, Harvey [19]), who have argued that the keep was not started until the second half of the 12th century.

The need for a castle does not invariably create the need for a priory, but Geoffrey had other concerns. Having been given and having established Kenilworth as his chief seat, he would have wanted to found some religious house there, as he put it, *for the redemption of his sins, and for the salvation of King Henry, his wife and children, and that of his own family and friends.* Like most of his contemporaries, he had high concern for the health and salvation of the soul.

At this time, the choice of Order was limited: Benedictine or Augustinian. The Benedictines had a hierarchical system of one house being founded from another, whereas Augustinian houses could be founded in line with the founder's wishes and requirements. It was fashionable for members of the court to found Augustinian houses; in fact, only two Benedictine houses were founded by members of Henry I's court, namely Reading, by Henry himself as his royal mausoleum, and another Benedictine Cluniac house at Farley, near Bath. Other attractive features were mentioned in Chapter I. Furthermore, it was not unusual for Augustinian houses to be founded near castles, and there are many examples of this, including Hastings and Porchester, where the Augustinian houses were within the castle walls, and in Warwickshire where the houses at Studley, Maxstoke, Kenilworth and Warwick are all adjacent to castles. From the point of view of the canons, the site was ideal: isolated, on the edge of a wilderness, but, at the same time, within the protection of the founder and his castle.

FOUNDATION

There are two basic foundation charters; one of Henry I, which, from its witnesses, can be dated between 1123 and 1129, granting Geoffrey land and confirming various grants to the canons. The other was Geoffrey de Clinton's own charter which can be more closely dated to 1126. A foundation charter

5

does not usually indicate the state of the house at the time, which may have been either when the idea was formalised, or when the first group of canons occupied it, or when the church was dedicated, or no more than when it was convenient to make a formal record. In the case of Kenilworth, however, Henry I's charter refers to lands that Geoffrey gave to Bernard the Prior (who is not mentioned in Geoffrey's charter); it might therefore be construed that Henry I's is the later, and that Bernard was perhaps appointed in the interim. In the case of Reading Abbey (Henry I's re-foundation on an existing priory), the abbot was appointed in April 1123, nearly two years after the monks had arrived, and the formal charter was drawn up two years later still. Periods between starting work and consecration of the church varied considerably – 17 years for Butley (Suffolk) and 23 years for Norton (Cheshire), both Augustinian. All that can be said for Kenilworth was that in the 1120's, it was not just a gleam in the eye, as a prior had been appointed, and building probably started.

Whilst granting the canons considerable lands and churches, detailed in Chapter VIII, the charters do not cover what was expected of the canons, unlike that for the Augustinian house of Maxstoke[15] of 1334, for instance, which states that the convent consists of an elected prior and 12 canons who are day and night to glorify God in their round of worship. As discussed in Chapter V, it is likely that the Kenilworth canons were expected to perform spiritual duties at the Castle and the new borough.

The Priory church was founded in honour of St Mary, and the Priory became known as St Mary the Virgin's, although, in one instance at least, St Augustine was implied in the dedication. St Mary, alone or in association with other saints, was by far the most popular spiritual patroness of priories and abbeys of all orders.

As indicated above, the building of a stone castle would have been given priority, perhaps with craftsmen only being diverted to the Priory as stages of the work were completed. From the late Romanesque chevron of the Chapter House, which might be compared with that of the Augustinian Chapter House of Bristol Cathedral (1142-70) or Iffley Church, Oxford, (1170-80), the Chapter House was completed c 1170, and the Church, usually the first stone building on site, somewhat earlier. Sleepy *Chinewrde* became a very busy place in the middle part of the 12th century, with two major buildings under construction, and quarrying in progress.

III PATRONAGE

Since the monastery of the Blessed Mary of Kenilworth, in
the County of Warwick, is of our foundation and patronage, ...

Henry VIII, in a charter of 3 November 1511

As founder of the Priory, Geoffrey de Clinton was also its patron, and this rôle descended through his heirs — in theory, at least. As founder, he was expected to grant the canons sufficient possessions to provide an adequate income, and this he did generously. In return the patron expected certain privileges.

At one time the patron considered himself to be the owner of the church or house he founded, but by the 12th Century, this was no longer the case. He could, however, claim hospitality for himself and his household. He could also require the canons to look after dependants or retired servants - *corrodians*. His permission usually had to be given for the election of a prior to take place, but at Kenilworth this was waived in the de Clinton's time; a bull of Honorius II issued in 1126 specifically absolved the Priory of this need. He had the important right of presenting the prior-elect to the bishop for approval and installation. He would also expect masses to be said for his spiritual welfare, both in life and after death, and for charity to be given in his name. Also, when the house was vacant, that is, between priors, the *Dominus Fundorum*, the founder and his successors, expected to receive some of the revenues.

The patronage of the de Clintons was relatively short-lived, however. The key to the change was almost certainly the tenure of Kenilworth Castle. The de Clintons had problems; in 1130, Geoffrey was accused of treason but nothing came of it (*see* Chapter XIV). He died not long after. Geoffrey II (Geoffrey's son) inherited Kenilworth but seems to have lost tenure of the Castle during the Anarchy (the reign of Stephen), but then regained it; in a charter of the period, he referred to the recovery of the Castle and his honour (the seignory of his manors). The Castle concerned may not have been Kenilworth, however, but the de Clintons' other Warwickshire castle at Brandon. It is arguable whether Geoffrey II's son, Henry, ever succeeded to the ownership of Kenilworth Castle. It was garrisoned by Henry II during the 1173-4 rebellion of his eldest son Henry, in which Henry de Clinton is claimed to have had complicity. Soon afterwards Henry was granted a manor at Lower Swansbourne, Buckinghamshire, in exchange for the Castle; it was recorded in the *Book of Fees*, that by 1242, the Abbot of Woburn held 480 acres (200 hectares) at Lower Swansbourne which were given to Henry de Clinton in exchange for Kenilworth Castle.

Geoffrey II died *c* 1170, but a charter of Henry II, probably a little earlier than this, is a notification that the church of St Mary, Kenilworth, (that is, the Priory) was held by the King and was in his protection. This may have been no more than a temporary arrangement during a vacancy of the priorship. On the other hand, it could indicate the stirrings of Royal interest in the patronage of the Priory.

Also at this time, Pope Alexander III (1159-81) notified the Prior and canons of Kenilworth that he had granted his 'protection' to their church and all its possessions. This was repeated by Gregory IX in May, 1238. The relevant part of Gregory IX's charter can be liberally translated as: *we take your church into our protection, including all the possessions you legitimately hold now and in the future, ... and that by our protection, we decree that neither your bishop, nor his officers, should make demands upon your churches, nor shall you be further burdened by unjust grievance. Therefore in the churches you hold, you are allowed to choose the clerks and to present them to the bishop of the diocese, and, if they are suitable, he will appoint them for the cure of souls; also that they are answerable to him on spiritual matters, but to you on temporal ones.* This is not, in fact, exemption from the bishop's rule, which for the Cistercian houses was quite usual. Dickinson [12] explains that *by 1100 it had become a well-established practice abroad for new houses to seek papal protection, and but that in England it was not until Pope Alexander III's time that there was a flood of such charters.* It therefore appears to have been merely a routine matter. In fact, as canons anciently originated under episcopal supervision, it would be a break with tradition for the canons to be 'exempt' from that supervision, although two Augustinian houses in special circumstances attained this status. These Papal charters probably resulted from some episcopal heavy-handedness somewhere.

Henry de Clinton's involvement with the Priory continued for a while; in 1196 he confirmed to the canons all the grants made by his grandfather, father and himself. In 1200, however, King John took charge of the Priory and put it in the hands of the archdeacon of Wells, Hugh de Wells and Hugh de Chaucumbe (Sheriff of Warwickshire 1206-7). But this again seems to have been a temporary arrangement pending the appointment of Prior Silvester in 1201/2. He was followed in 1203 by Prior Walter, but by 1208, Walter was deposed *for many excesses* and the King put the Priory in the care of a layman, one Henry de Cerne. He held it for five years, during at least some of which time the payments due to the *domini fundorum*, presumably still the de Clintons, continued.

March 1208 saw Pope Innocent III place England under the Interdict; no prior was appointed and Henry de Cerne still managed the house's affairs. The King was excommunicated in 1209, and the Interdict not raised until John had submitted to the Pope in 1212. Stephen Langton, consecrated Archbishop of Canterbury by the Pope in 1207, had to remain on the Continent until 1213. On returning and taking up office, he seems to have questioned both Henry de Clinton and Richard, Prior of Stafford, on the procedure for the appointment of Kenilworth priors. Whatever the precise question, Richard replied that, from foundation, the canons had themselves chosen their priors without anyone's consent, and Henry replied that during a vacancy, the family did not claim the custody of the Priory, but that they had the right of presentation of the new prior to the bishop. This, incidentally, seems to have been the last involvement of Henry de Clinton in the Priory's affairs. Meanwhile, King John instructed Alexander Nequam, John Hastings and the Constable of the Castle to accompany the Archbishop of Canterbury's Clerk to enquire into the rights regarding election at Kenilworth. It would seem that the Priory had now become a focus of royal attention.

The next year, 1214, Master Henry de Cerne, still the custodian of the Priory, was informed that William de Barton, the sub-prior of the Oxfordshire Augustinian house of Oseney, had been appointed Prior of Kenilworth. This was the turning point and from there on, until the Dissolution, it was the Crown's right to license the canons to elect a prior, and then to approve their choice. Thus, on 4 September 1227, Henry III, from Windsor, gave the canons licence to elect their prior. He went further, limiting their choice from among brothers Richard, Osbert and Stephen, but this was ignored, however, as on the 11 September, still at Windsor, the King gave his royal assent to the canons' choice of Henry, the sub-prior. Thereafter, whenever the Priory became vacant, that is to say the Prior had resigned or died, a letter from the Chapter was taken to the King by two or three canons, requesting licence to elect a new prior. The King then appointed a guardian of the Priory. For example, on the resignation of Prior David in 1259, the King's clerk, Henry de Malo Lacu, was appointed on 4 May and continued until after 1 July when royal assent was given to the election of Prior Nicholas.

During a voidance – a vacant priorship – the king received the temporalities of the Priory (revenues from land, etc), providing him, perhaps, with an incentive to prolong it. Kenilworth, however, was given release from this in 1330 when it was decreed that when vacant, the Sub-prior should hold custody of the Priory together with all the revenues except the Knights' service and the advowsons of the churches, valued at £117 2s 8d, which the Crown claimed. This concession was in consideration of the expenses incurred by the Priory during frequent visits of Edward II and the reigning King, Edward III, to the Priory. The implication is that these visits were not passing occasions, but ones where significant hospitality was claimed, as befitted a royal patron.

This procedure for election was followed into the 16th century. It seems that the Bishop of Coventry & Lichfield had little say in this process, except that he sent a letter to the King confirming the vacancy, as in 1236, and received notification of the Royal assent to the choice, as in 1345. An indication of the relationships between Pope, Bishop and Prior might be gleaned from a papal mandate of 1290. It appears that the Prior had complained to the Pope as a result of which the Pope had instructed the diocesan Bishop that, when he visited the Priory, he was not to bring secular (that is, unprofessed) members of his retinue into the enclosure (Inner Court), and that he was to be accompanied by no more than two or three of his canons, in fitting habit. The Priory may not have been exempt, but papal protection seems to have had its worth. The Bishop was, in fact, required to visit his diocesan houses every three years, but from the limited records that have been transcribed, it appears that Bishop Stretton, for instance, only made one visit in his 27 years as Bishop. This was the well-known occurrence in 1361, when, at the special direction of the King, the Bishop ordered the Prior and convent to assemble in the chapter house on 21 June, as the unsatisfactory state of the house had become notorious. The outcome is not known, but the Prior, John de Peyto, was dead by July; he may well have been a victim of the plague of that year. On the other hand, there are records of Bishop Geoffrey Blythe's visits in 1496, 1518, 1521 and 1524.

It was not rare for the Crown to be the founder and patron of an Augustinian house; Henry I founded the houses of Carlisle, Cirencester, Dunstable, Southampton and Wellow (Lincs), and was associated with the founding of several others. Kenilworth seems unique in that the Crown assumed patronage at a later date. Did John, with the sun going down on the de Clintons' fortunes, justify his action on the grounds that the original land was granted by Henry I, and was, perhaps, Geoffrey de Clinton only regarded as an instrument?

The Abbey seal (Catalogue No M417 [16], Figure 9), appended to a deed on 17 March, 1538, has the seated Virgin with Child on her knee, below which are the Royal Arms as used in the period from 1405 to 1603.

The effect of Royal Patronage on the Priory was significant. The Prior was expected to provide royal hospitality, and to provision the King, as during the 1266 siege of Kenilworth Castle when the Priory provided the King with 300 quarters of corn 'and other things'. The King's retainers were sent to be looked after at the Priory as corrodians. In 1317, Alice, whose husband Henry Morton had served the King well in Scotland, was sent to the Priory for maintenance as a free servant. In 1327, Thomas le Veutrer replaced John Powys, deceased, as a corrodian, and in 1330, Nicholas de Veutrer replaced Walter Joice, who had also died. In addition, each newly appointed abbot and prior had to maintain a King's clerk until a benefice or living had been found for him. Thus on the election of Abbot Walle, Richard Dolphyn was given the allowance due from an abbot elect, for an unspecified period.

The King also had the right to appoint the vicars to the canons' churches when the priorship itself was vacant. In 1279, between the priorship of William de Evesham and Richard de Tynesford, the rector of Chesterton and the vicar of Lillington were appointed by the king as patron. Likewise, in 1361, the King held the patronage of Leek Wootton church due to a vacant priorship.

The King not only acquired the patronage, but also the title of 'founder'. In 1361, after Prior John de Peyto died, Edward III, as *patron and founder*, gave the necessary licence for his successor, Henry de Bradweye, to be elected. Also Henry VIII, in a charter licensing the Priory to purchase land in Mortmain, also addressed himself as *'founder and patron'*. The de Clintons' rôle had been well and truly usurped!

IV THE ESTABLISHMENT

... let there be one elected prior, and a convent of
twelve canons in addition to the prior..

Concerning the number of canons,
Maxstoke foundation charter

The average number of canons in Augustinian houses in England was twelve rising to seventeen by the early 13th Century. This was small compared with the great houses; the Benedictine monastery of Christchurch, Canterbury, held 150 monks in 1125; Oseney, just outside Oxford, appears as the largest Augustinian house with 50 canons in 1225 and 1325, the number falling to about 20 at the Dissolution. In the late 15th and early 16th centuries there were 16 - 19 canons and novices at Kenilworth, but there is little positive information for other times. Prof Knowles[23] states that Augustinian establishments were usually founded with a fixed complement; 13 for a smaller house and 26 for a larger, into which category he put Kenilworth. The origin of thirteen is, of course, the Master and the twelve Apostles, and the Cistercians and Benedictines adopted this number as a 'full convent' or minimum establishment.

Figure 3 is a histogram of the <u>average</u> number of canons in Augustinian houses over the period 1125 to the Dissolution. It shows a rise, peaking at *c* 1225, then gently declining until the Black Death in 1349 when it dips. Thereafter, the number remains approximately constant. Dugdale[14] lists 14 Kenilworth canons receiving pensions at the Dissolution; he also lists 16 whom he implies as present at the surrender of the Abbey on 29 April, 1538. The Table at the end of this chapter details the establishment for Bishop Geoffrey Blythe's visits in 1518, 1521 and 1524, showing 17 - 19 canons and novices.

The Constitutions of Pope Benedict required houses to send one out of every twenty members to a university – one fit to acquire the fruits of greater learning. At the triennial General Chapter of the Order of Augustinians[31] in 1443, Kenilworth was fined, together with 32 other houses, for failing to send a scholar to university, implying Kenilworth had more than 20 canons. The fine was actually £10 for each defaulting year since the previous Chapter, some houses being fined the full £30. Kenilworth was fined only £20, implying that in one of the three previous years, a student had been supported – or the number had then been less than 20. There is a *caveat* on this conclusion, however, as Visitors, appointed by the General Chapter, could require a house to comply if it had sufficient income, regardless of size. Kenilworth was not a poor house, and may have fallen into this category. Nevertheless, there is a case for assuming that Kenilworth had more than 20 canons in 1443 – about twice the average.

On the assumption that the Kenilworth establishment followed the general trend, then in the peak period of

the early 13th century, there were 25 canons, close to Knowles' 26. This is in accord with the church being modified and extended in order to cope with a larger number of canons (Pevsner[28] gives an unsourced date of 1276 for work being in progress, and recent archæological studies have provided some support for this).

On the basis of this evidence, therefore, Kenilworth may have been founded for 13 canons, but was uprooted to 26 in the 13th century. So far, 177 canons, abbots and priors have been identified, *see* 'Who's Who'.

Servants allowed the canons to concentrate on their spiritual duties. No record remains of these at Kenilworth, but from an analysis of data from three other Warwickshire houses at the Dissolution, conveniently recorded by Dugdale, it is found that the canons and novices averaged some 23% of the total establishment. This agrees well with a value of 22.4% derived from 41 male houses where the number of religious was 487 (monks and canons), employing 1685 lay servants (quoted by Savine, 1909). Basing Kenilworth on, say, 16 – 20 canons, the estimated total establishment was 70 – 87 persons, including yeomen, farm workers, dairy maids, servants and corrodians.

MANAGEMENT

'The Barnwell Observances'[8], the rules of an important Cambridgeshire Augustinian priory, show that the organisation of Augustinian houses was much like those of any monastic order. The details are available of the visits to Kenilworth by Bishop Geoffrey Blythe in 1518, 1521 and 1524; these contain both the names of the canons and their rôles, shown in the table below. The Officers, or 'Obedientiaries' were appointed by the Prior, following discussion beforehand at meetings of the Chapter. The rôles of these officers are broadly as follows. (Those of the Prior and Abbot are discussed in Chapter VI.)

The <u>Sub-prior</u> was the officer next to the prior; as well as acting as superior in the prior's absence, he was also responsible for conduct and discipline. He held an important rôle as the buffer between the prior and the brethren; it was a post requiring some tact. There was an alleged case in 1426 of the Sub-prior being contumacious to the Prior, but as discussed under Stone in Chapter X, the details are blurred. On attaining abbatial rank, the prior undertook the duties of sub-prior.

The <u>Cellarer</u> was the prior's right hand man on temporal matters. He was responsible for the material welfare of the brethren and managed the priory's estates, the lay brethren being responsible to him. One cellarer, at least, became prior.

The Precentor was the Cellarer's counterpart on the spiritual side. He was responsible for the conduct of the ritual and the library. The Succentor was his assistant. The Sacristan had the care of the church and its contents, even to the extent of having to sleep in it to guard it. The Master of the Fermery (we would call the Fermery the 'sick-bay' or the 'Infirmary') looked after the sick, the Almoner after the poor and aged, the Fraterer the refectory, and the Kitchener, of course, the kitchen.

At some time, and it is not apparent why and when, lay officers of the Abbey were appointed. In 1534, Henry, Marquis of Dorset, was High Steward with an annual fee of £5 6s 8d; Laurence Grey was Receiver General with £6 a year and John Lodbrok, Auditor, with £2 13s 4d. The rôle of the High Steward, at least, was somewhat of a sinecure, mainly furthering the monastery's influence at Court, several stewardships often being held by one notable.

VISITS BY BISHOP GEOFFREY BLYTHE

BROTHERS	1518	1521	1524
WALL, William	Abbot	Abbot	Abbot
ORWELL, Robert	Prior	Prior	Prior
LYSTER, John	Sub-prior	Sub-prior	Sub-prior
RUTH, Henry	Ill	Ill with gout	-
TYLLY, Richard	Sacrist	Sacrist	Sacrist
ROGERS, John	Canon	Canon	Canon
LICHFIELD, John	Abbot's Chaplain	Abbot's Chaplain	Abbot's Chaplain
ROGERS, Richard	Treasurer	Cellarer	Cellarer/Kitchener
BOLTON, Hugo	Almoner	Almoner	Almoner
PENKETH, John	Cellarer	-	-
BONDE, Edmund	Fraterer	Kitchener	Kitchener
ALCESTRE, Robert	Fermery Master	Fermery Master	Fermery Master
BADGER, Richard	Canon	Sub-sacrist	Sub-sacrist
LEYCESTRE, William	Novice	Fraterer	-
COVENTRY, Thomas	Novice	Succentor	Precentor
STONE, Thomas	Novice	Novice	Master of Novices
YARDLEY, Ralph	Novice	Novice	Novice
STONELEY, Thomas	-	Novice	Novice
HARWELL, Roger	-	Novice	Novice
JEKES (or Jekys), Simon	-	Novice	Novice
TOTAL RELIGIOUS	13 + 4 novices	14 + 5 novices	13 + 4 novices

AVERAGE
NUMBER OF CANONS IN
AUGUSTINIAN
ESTABLISHMENTS

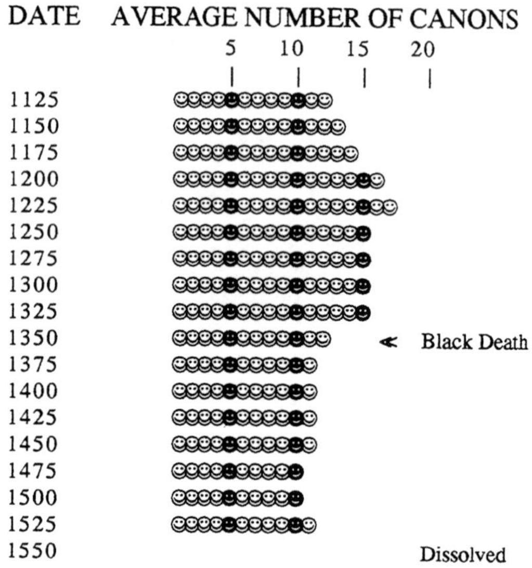

DATE	AVERAGE NUMBER OF CANONS			
	5	10	15	20
1125				
1150				
1175				
1200				
1225				
1250				
1275				
1300				
1325				
1350			← Black Death	
1375				
1400				
1425				
1450				
1475				
1500				
1525				
1550	Dissolved			

Based on Data for 116 houses from Robinson[30]

FIG 3

A CANON REGULAR OF ST AUGUSTINE

(From a print in the abridged version of *Monasticon Anglicanum*,
Sam Keeble, 1692)

FIG 4

V THE COMMON LIFE

Before all else, live together in harmony,
being of one mind and heart on the way to God.
For is this not precisely the reason that
you have come to live together?

The Rule of St Augustine

ADMINISTRATION OF THE RULE

Any specific rules for Kenilworth have long since been lost, but an overall view of the life of the canons can be drawn from other sources, although it is important to realise that over four centuries there was scope for change – generally towards relaxation.

The order was popular because of the latitude that could be applied to the interpretation of the Augustinian Rule. However, the Lateran Council of 1215, in the quest for uniformity, ordered a three-yearly meeting of the superiors of every order within a kingdom or province. Thus two General Chapters of the Order of St Augustine were formed, one for the northern province (York), and one for the southern (Canterbury), although they combined in 1341. At the Chapter of 1234, it was decreed that every house should have its written rules for the instruction of novices. The Chapters introduced new rules from time to time, and in 1339, Benedict XII issued his Constitutions for the Black Canons.

The Constitutions were more or less inflexible, but there still remained a degree of freedom within houses as to the extent to which the rules were applied. One house might have been famed for scholarship, as this is what they they saw as being the right thing to do; another might have been contemplative and yet another may have concentrated on parochial work in a city. The Sussex house of Pynham, near Arundel, was founded for the express purpose of maintaining a crossing of the river Arun!

The Augustinian Chapter also nominated Diocesan Visitors who reported back to the General Chapter on the state of the houses, thus ensuring some level of uniformity. Instructions were issued on how to conduct such visitations, detailing what was, and what was not, expected. The bishop was also required to visit the houses in his diocese every three years, although this did not always take place.

Barnwell Priory, as we have seen, had very detailed rules [8], drawn up in 1295/6. Nearer to home, there is the 1337 Foundation Charter [15] of the Warwickshire house of Maxstoke, which again throws light on the canons' life. These have been used for the following.

RECRUITMENT

Under the Assize of Clarendon, of 1166, Henry II forbade the reception of any man of low degree (*de populo minuto*) as a monk, canon or friar by any house, until his character had been established – unless he was at death's door. (The previous Constitutions of Clarendon of 1164 had barred the sons of 'rustics' from being ordained without the consent of the lord in whose land they were born; this, seemingly, was more to protect the lord from the loss of villeins, for whom life in the cloister could only be an improvement, than to raise the standard of the clergy.)

The novice had to stem from a good background and be at least 18 years old, honest and a freeman at the time of entry, without any impediment to becoming a canon and a priest, such as illegitimacy. In 1290, the Pope commissioned the Bishop of Coventry and Lichfield to grant a dispensation, because of illegitimate birth, to allow two Kenilworth canons to become priests. The novice needed a good singing voice and sufficient learning (including, of course, literacy) to become a canon. On being accepted and given his habit, he served a year's probation under the master of novices. On becoming a professed canon, vows of poverty, chastity and obedience were taken.

Only two examples have been found of minor orders being taken, that is, those of 'doorkeeper', 'exorcist', 'lector' and 'acolyte'; Roger de Hynham and John de Whitchurch were both ordained acolytes. This seems unusual – at an ordination in 1309 by the suffragan Bishop of Worcester, 210 acolytes were ordained, but not one was from a religious house, suggesting that such ordinations were not usual for canons and monks. On the other hand, the Abbot of Oseney had the Papal privilege of conferring minor orders on novices.

There is plenty of evidence that the recruits progressed through the higher orders of sub-deacon and deacon to priesthood, which they were all required to attain. Ordinations by the bishop or his representative took place five times a year, one such taking place at Kenilworth Priory in 1340 when 83 sub-deacons, 112 deacons and 37 priests were ordained. Priesthood could not be conferred on a candidate until he was 24 years old, and, as Bishop Robert Stretton of Coventry & Lichfield warned, *he must not be a married or bigamous man, nor illegitimate, unless legitimised by the Apostolic See;* also candidates had to be examined by his Clerk, *and let them that disregard, beware.* At the Augustinian house at Bristol, the minimum age for priesthood was lowered to 22 by Pope Urban V because of a shortfall due to the Black Death, just as he gave permission to the Prior of Kenilworth for four of his 22-year-old canons to be ordained in 1369.

Canons' names (see 'Who's Who') betray their place of origin. Some have the names of cells of Kenilworth – Richard de Brok (Brook) and Roger Stone, and also Richard Hethe, the canons having the advowson of the church at Hethe (Oxon). Many other names have a local ring – John de Coventry, Thomas Stoneley, Richard Warewick and Thomas de Warmington. Others have names from further afield – William de Evesham, Roger Harwell, John Lichfield and Thomas Rockester.

One of the early canons was the second son of Geoffrey de Clinton, Robert de Clinton. Robert's brother, Geoffrey II, endowed the canons with the church of Packington for his 'reception' – the only example found of a 'dowry' being provided. In 1124 the Earl of Warwick claimed the right to have a canon of his nomination at Kenilworth, in return for granting the canons the churches of Brailes and Wellesbourne, and certain land. The possibility of recruitment from among the parish priests has been sought [35], but so far only a William Wall, priest at Stoneleigh in 1494, has been found who might be the same person as William Walle, a Kenilworth canon who first appears in 1509, and later became Abbot.

———— † ————

LIFE IN THE CLOISTER

SPIRITUAL LIFE: The convent life was dominated by the 'Hours', which all canons, including the prior and officers, had to attend, unless there was a reasonable cause to be absent. The period of daylight was divided into 12 hours of length dependent on the season, and a time-table arranged.

THE HOURS:

The Monastic Day (Summer)

MIDNIGHT	Matins and Lauds after which the canons return to the dorter and sleep until the bell rings for:
SUNRISE	Prime
Hours 1-3	Morning Mass followed by private Masses and Confessions, meeting of the Chapter and then work. Terce
Hours 4-6	High Mass and Sext, followed by reading until Dinner, at which the Scriptures are read.
MID-DAY	Rest in Dorter until bell for:-
Hours 7-9	Nones followed by hand-washing and a drink in Frater. Then work until:-
Hours 10-12	Evensong Supper. Then servants eat whilst Convent read in Cloister, until bell rings for:-
SUNSET	Collation, Compline and bed

Silence was observed generally (except in the event of *accident, namely robbers or thieves, sickness, fire and workmen*), and specifically in the refectory, and in the cloister at times that *are fitting and customary*. The exceptions appear to have been during any hiatus after Chapter, and in the summer, when the brethren were allowed to talk on the west side of the cloister between Nones and Evensong. Then, and whenever silence was to be broken, the Sub-prior would say *Benedicite*, the convent replying *Dominum*. Necessary discussion could take place in the Parlour or wherever other brothers would not be distracted. The General Chapter of the Order decreed in 1325 that if it was necessary to speak during the hours of silence, then only Latin or French should be spoken.

FOOD AND DRINK: On the matter of food, the Rule stated *keep bodily appetites in check by fasting and abstinence from food according to needs*, but custom varied throughout the order. The Rule of St Benedict demanded abstinence, except by the sick, from the meat of four-footed beasts, although secular canons, from whom the Augustinians were derived, had no ban on meat. One of the early charters of Geoffrey de Clinton was to grant them pasture for their animals and their pigs. In 1291, they were also granted free warren of their lands at Kenilworth, Packington and Idlicote and, in 1388, at Salford, Radford, Ettington and Hughenden in Berkshire. Free warren was the right to breed and hunt beasts and fowl of the warren, including roes, hare, *conie* (rabbit), pheasant, partridge, quail, rail, woodcock, mallard and *herne* (heron). Geoffrey also granted them a tenth of all produce going into the castle, and this included corn, hay, hogs, muttons, bacon, venison, cheese, fish, wine, honey wax, tallow, pepper and cummin. At the Augustinian Priory of Norton, Cheshire, *thousands of bones were found in the excavations*. Prime cuts of beef were the most popular, but it must be appreciated that the canons also had to extend high levels of hospitality at times, so they were not necessarily the recipients. The canons themselves were not permitted to hunt, and more than one house was censured by the bishop for keeping hunting dogs. There were also periods of fasting: Lent (seven weeks) and Advent (four weeks), and a weekly fast on the 'sixth day' – Friday, the day of Crucifixion. Fasting consisted of bread and water only, according to the notes for Visitors appointed by the Order.

The canons had permission to fish the Castle Mere on Thursdays and they developed their own pools along the valley of Finham Brook. Kenilworth, incidentally, was renowned for its bream - carp was only introduced to England about 1500. Oyster shells have recently been reported in the stream alongside the Abbey site; these were, of course, common fare in mediæval times, and have also been found at the Castle, having been brought considerable distances from the coast.

Beer was available to the canons. In 1196, they granted Henry de Clinton 2 loaves daily and 4 gallons of better beer in return for his confirmation of their possessions. In 1306, the Prior paid a wine bill of the huge amount of £19.14s.0d, inflated, no doubt, by providing Edward I with heavy hospitality, for which concessions were given to the Priory (*see* Chapter III).

HEALTH: According to the Barnwell Observances, each brother had to be bled seven times a year. This was presumably for health reasons, to curb carnal desire and allow the mind to concentrate; according to the Chronicles of Evesham[10], Nicholas of Tusculum, the Papal Legate, came to England in 1213 to raise the Interdict; he also went to Evesham to investigate the Abbot's conduct. Finding him wanting, he dismissed him; he then bled himself, and called a meeting in the chapter house for four days hence for the election of a new Abbot. When bled, a canon normally spent three days in the fermery, when rules were suspended. One good meal a day, and conversation was freely allowed; but games unsuitable for a religious life, such as dice and chess, were specifically forbidden.

USE OF BUILDINGS: The Dorter, or dormitory, was a place of quiet and secrecy, where the head and face had to be hidden in the hoods, especially when going to the rere-dorter (latrine). Monks, at least, are associated with having cells, certainly the Carthusians, who led a totally isolated life in them. In the case of the canons, whilst the dormitory was open plan in the early stages, by the 16th century, if not long before, each canon had his own cubicle.

There would have been a library, run by the Precentor, and almost certainly, a *scriptorium.* There is no evidence either way that the Kenilworth canons wrote or copied books, but they had need, at least, to prepare and copy the many charters and letters that were essential for the affairs of the house.

All the brethren, even the sick, unless too ill, had to take part in processions on Sundays and other solemn occasions. The Sunday procession round the cloister was led by the bearer of holy water, then followed the cross and tapers, the sub-deacon with book, the deacon, and, finally, the Celebrant. These were followed by the convent, the juniors first, and the canons in pairs, at intervals of four feet, with the prior taking up the rear. On Wednesdays and Fridays in Lent, there were processions, the canons walking barefooted. On Easter Day, Ascension, Pentecost, the Assumption and on the days appropriate to St Mary, to whom the convent was dedicated, they processed with a shrine or reliquary, and on All Souls' day, the cemetery was included in the route. Kings, archbishops and bishops were met with processions, which were also held to intercede for rain, fine weather and peace.

CLOTHES AND DRESS: An idea of dress can be gained from Figure 4, a print of a Canon Regular of St Augustine, based on one by Wenceslaus Hollar who created a number of prints in the early 17th century. The long, black, sheepskin-lined cassock (the *pellicea)* was the distinguishing mark of the Augustinians, giving them the name 'The Black Canons'. On liturgical occasions, this was covered by

a white linen *rochet* with wide sleeves. A black cloak or cope (*cappa*) was worn over the cassock when the canons left the monastery. Geoffrey de Clinton decreed that all the lambskins from all his manors, regardless of whether they died naturally or were killed for food, were to be given to the canons for their apparel. Nonetheless, distinguishing features of canons and monks were that canons wore linen rather than wool, and they remained bearded.

Matters of dress were discussed by the General Chapter of the Order: in 1334, it was decreed that canons should wear blue capes, and in 1359, that they should wear gaiters, not close hose; in 1374, shoes and close-fitting hose were banned in preference for jack-boots or gaiters, as it appears that canons were known on occasions to lift their habits up to the knees to show off their calves!

HYGIENE: The Augustinians brought to England not only a more vigorous monasticism but also a new standard of monastic hygiene that had been lacking in their Benedictine forebears until this time. To an Augustinian, uncleanliness *was a sin of negligence, not a sign of goodness.* The Rule states: *because bathing may be necessary for good health, the opportunity to visit public baths may never be refused. Even if a person is unwilling, he shall do what has to be done for the good of his health, if necessary at the command of the superior. But if someone wants to go bathing just because he enjoys it ..... he will have to learn to renounce his desires. For what a person likes may not always be good for him. It may even be harmful.*

CONDUCT: The priory was not to be left without the prior's permission, especially before canons could visit a tavern. The Rule required all canons to proceed in pairs outside the monastery.

On manual and other labours, the rule says little, but a 12th century document from the Augustinian house of Bridlington, the *Bridlington Dialogue,* lists the skills that canons should practise: *Reading, explaining or preaching the word of God before the brethren; practising for divine worship either by reading or singing: preparing parchment for the writers, writing, illuminating, ruling lines, scoring music, correcting and binding books; sewing new clothes for the brethren and repairing old ones; making wooden spoons and candlesticks and the like: fashioning baskets, nets and beehives, and weaving mats. And to come to outside pursuits both to dig and dung the garden, to lay out the garden beds, sow seeds of vegetables and herbs, to plant and water vegetables and herbs, trim and prune, graft and move trees – and so on.*

It hardly need be said that the canons were to avoid women, although there is clear evidence that, at the Dissolution (*sic*), there were women servants at the Warwickshire Augustinian houses of Maxstoke and Studley. The Visitor was required to investigate whether there were any pregnant women within the confines of the house.

The general behaviour of the canons had to be much as we would expect of them today. Among the 'thou shalt nots' listed was the carrying of weapons, planning crimes, becoming involved in secular business, embracing women, dancing and improper singing, and owning personal property.

Each canon was required to celebrate Mass daily on behalf of his brethren and past priors. This explains the multiplicity of chapels in the transepts.

———— † ————

As suggested earlier, there was a general relaxation of the rules during the passage of time. One can imagine the early canon living the full common life, sharing all. By the 16th century, however, they received salaries for the purchase of their own clothes, &c, and had their own garden plots. Guyot de Provins, a minstrel who became a monk, summed up the trend, perhaps a little wickedly, by saying of the canons regular in the 13th century: *Augustin, whose rule they allow, was more courteous than Benedict. Among them* (the Augustinians), *one is well shod, well cloathed, well fed. They go out when they like, mix with the world, and talk at table.*

CHAPTER

The 'agenda' of the daily meeting in the Chapter House is evident from the records of Barnwell[8] and the Augustinian house of St Victor, Paris. Chapter took place in the first half of the morning, after Mass. The brethren, including, it seems, novices and lay brethren assembled on the ringing of the bell. The Psalms and part of the Rule were read, followed by general announcements. The precentor then read the Table for the week – the duties of certain canons at services. After a sermon by the prior, all lay-brethren and novices left. The precentor went over the services for the next 24 hours, rehearsing what was to be said or sung. The prior then invited any canon whose conscience troubled him to come forward and ask pardon for his fault. Canons could then make charges against each other, confessing and asking for pardon if guilty. Punishment included flogging, there and then. Stripped to the waist, the offender was flogged, not by his accuser but by an equal or superior, until the prior signalled it was to cease. Another form of punishment was to be sent to the cell at Brooke, for instance, or even to another house of the order. There is no evidence that Kenilworth had a dungeon, although this was recommended by the Chapter of the Order. No mention was to be made outside Chapter of the secret business that took place within.

Temporal matters were then considered; the appointment of officers, reception of novices, grant of corrodies, the signing of deeds with the fixing of the priory seal by common consent, and dealing with all correspondence etc. Business with outsiders could also be conducted in the Chapter House. In 1316, the canons ordained a Chantry at Ettington for the souls of Thomas, Earl of Lancaster *et al;* the priest appointed to the chantry was required to make an oath of fidelity in the Chapter House at Kenilworth.

Like every successful community, the canons needed a set of rules that minimised discord. In time, however, the rules became more relaxed, and a recent study by the authors of the Bishop's representative's visitations in the early 16th century shows dissension and polarisation of views among the canons.

VI THE EXTERNAL ROLE

Acknowledgement that the Prior of Kenilleworth has paid £20,
which he promised against the king's crossing into Gascony.

Patent Rolls, 17 May, 1242

S o far, only the 'cloister' activities of the canons have been considered. Besides these, however, they had to administer the source of their income – their churches and lands – and the superior in particular had wide duties outside the convent. The following explores how far they were involved with the outside world.

THE CANONS & THEIR CHURCHES

The most pertinent question is whether the canons serviced the churches under their control – or indeed any churches, apart, of course, from their own priory church. Dickinson[12] has addressed this question as far as the whole of the English order is concerned, and after lengthy analysis he states that *'as far as the vast majority of houses, at least, were concerned, there was never any intention that the early inmates should undertake the care of most or all the parishes given to them.'* At Worksop, for instance, the nave of the canons' church was the parish church, but this had its own nominated parish priests, albeit a few of them being canons.

The general evidence for Kenilworth is that the canons presented their nominated priests to the Bishop of Coventry and Lichfield, where their churches lay in his diocese, and to the Bishop of Worcester for the remainder of Warwickshire (*see* Appendix for details of these dioceses) and appropriate bishops elsewhere. Apart from taking their portion of the tithe, they left them to provide the cure of souls. The list of vicars for their adjacent church of St Nicholas is more or less complete, and there is no evidence of bolstering by the Priory, nor is there in any other of their Warwickshire churches. The canons, in any case, did not have the resources to service their 21 churches in Warwickshire with only a probable maximum of 25 canons, many of whom were committed to home-bound duties. On the other hand they may have carried out pastoral duties from time to time – when one of their churches was vacant, for instance – and then all the tithes would be received by the Priory, as its patron.

Outside the county, there were exceptions, however. The Kenilworth canons held the patronage of the church of All Saints at Brooke in Rutland and it was laid down that it had to be served by either a canon of Kenilworth or of Brooke, a cell of Kenilworth; another variation occurred at the canons' church at Ellastone, adjacent to their cell at Calwich, Staffordshire. Here, in 1298, Robert, a canon of

Kenilworth, was the nominated vicar. Generally, the situation seems as Dickinson has stated.

That does not mean to say that the canons just sat there, waiting for the tithes to roll in. The temporal aspects of the churches in their appropriation (*see* Chapter VII) were their responsibility; not only did these churches require repair, but, like all parish churches, they were enlarged from time to time. The responsibility for the nave was the responsibility of the communities the churches served, but the chancel was the responsibility of the rector who, in the case of appropriated churches, was the convent as the patron.

There were also other broader duties, such as when there was bloodshed in the churchyard of the canons' church at Kineton; the Bishop of Worcester, in whose diocese it was, ordered them 'to reconcile it with Holy Water'.

Another important question is whether the canons provided the spiritual needs of the Castle – and Geoffrey de Clinton's borough, which lacked its own parish church. Shortly after founding the Priory, Geoffrey de Clinton confirmed the canons' right to a tithe on everything that came into the Castle, but it does not follow that they provided a service in return. On the other hand, the Castle had two chapels, but the Bishop's Registers do not show any appointments of priests to them; thus it is reasonable to suppose that the canons served their local Castle, as probably did their counterparts from the other four Warwickshire Augustinian houses serve their nearby castles.

The one and only mention of canons at the Castle is a curious one. In 1318, Thomas, Earl of Lancaster, Steward of England, built and endowed a chapel of St Mary in the Castle, near the later Leicester buildings. This chapel, he stipulated, was to be served by thirteen secular canons; in other words, he was intending to set up a collegiate church. His plan, however, was cut short by his attainder and execution. Why did he wish to set up a college of canons? Had he fallen out with the canons regular, as has been suggested? Or had the Kenilworth canons become so introspective that they were no longer prepared to leave their church and cloister to provide a service to the Castle?

The question also arises as to whether the canons ran a school. The Augustinians had the reputation of being a scholastic order, having powered the first university organisation at Oxford; Thomas Becket was educated at Merton Priory, an Augustinian House averaging 23 canons, of similar size to Kenilworth. Another house, Bushmead (Bucks), which seems to have had only 4 canons, was licensed to keep a school of 60 boys and teach them *science of grammar* (*sic*). Some Augustinian houses had schools for poor boys in the Almonry; Barnwell, for instance, and Leicester Abbey, where up to 25 boys were accommodated. Is it therefore likely that Kenilworth had such a school – perhaps for the sons of the Castle's retinue – in which case, may it have been in the Castle, run by canons?

There was also responsibility towards the poor. The Almoner had all the scraps from the frater, the prior's chambers and the Guest House for distribution to the poor. On Maundy Thursday, as many poor men as there were canons were brought into the cloister for the washing of feet and to receive from each canon one penny.

THE ROLE OF THE SUPERIOR

'*Superior*' is a convenient and legitimate term to use to cover both prior and abbot. The Superior was not just the head of the house, but he had a separate secular rôle as well. The bringing of the Priory under royal patronage brought some special duties with it. With the raising of the Priory to an Abbey, these would have been extended.

Elected by his peers (with the King's licence, &c) the Superior led the house in all aspects of its life. He selected the officers, after discussion with the senior canons. He extracted respect – a bow, for instance, from any canon who passed him. He was expected to lead in many of the services, set an example by eating with the brethren and sleeping in the dormitory. As his duties became more onerous, especially in the field of entertainment, he had his own room, and later on, probably a Prior's/Abbot's House for entertaining important guests.

The Superior had his own chaplain which he was supposed to change annually (but John Lichfield seems to have been Abbot's Chaplain from before 1515 to after 1524, apparently without break). Each canon was required to make his confession directly to the Superior at least once a year. The Superior had to present an annual set of accounts for approval by the canons in Chapter.

The variety of the rôle of the Superior outside the convent can best be gleaned from instances given below.

Lord of the Manor

In a charter of *c* 1135, Geoffrey de Clinton II confirmed his father's grants to the canons, and stated that they shall have their court, customs and liberties just as freely as he had. It was also recorded in 1473, that the canons had power to keep Court Leet, the manorial court, the Assize of Bread and Beer (at which prices were fixed) and the authority to try malefactors. In other words, the canons had full manorial rights, and hence the Superior was one of the two Lords of the Manor of Kenilworth, that of the Castle Manor being whoever held the Castle at the time. These privileges covered a number of manors,

and the full extent of the superior's control is dealt with in Chapter VIII.

In 1322, Prior Thomas de Warmington become the receiver of the issues and honour of Kenilworth. This was in place of the previously mentioned Thomas, Earl of Lancaster, Lord of the Castle Manor, captured at the battle of Boroughbridge and executed without trial. Thus Prior Thomas became Lord of both the Kenilworth manors. This was only a temporary situation, however, as by 1324, Edward II had restored the castle and manor to Thomas' brother Henry, only to become his prisoner at Kenilworth in 1326.

Agent

In 1225, together with the Archdeacon of Coventry, Prior William Barton was required to force the Abbey and Convent of St Mary's, York (Benedictine) to hand over all documentation with respect to their indulgences and privileges, which were thought to be false.

In 1252, with the Prior of St Sepulchre's, Warwick, Prior David was required to prohibit, in the King's name, any tournament that was to be held in Warwick. Also, in 1271, Henry de Bradweye, in the company of the Abbot of Alcester (Benedictine) had to go to Warwick to show the King's ban on a tournament to be held on the day after Epiphany.

Banker with Safe Deposit

In 1173, the chirograph (deed) of one of the claimants in a case was given to the Prior for safe custody, the claimant having no safe place of her own. In 1257 the Barons of the Exchequer were ordered to find out what had happened to various rolls containing court decisions that had been made by the Justices. As a result, the Abbot of Leicester and the Prior of Kenilworth were asked to send in any rolls they held of the judgements of Stephen de Seagrave, an outstanding judge of his period and a Sheriff of Warwickshire. In the case of the Baddesley Clinton Estate, which had descended to two co-heiresses in 1530, the title deeds were placed in a chest with two locks and deposited with Abbot William Wall for safe-keeping and for reference by either party on request.

Money raised from the Jewry in Warwick for the King's use in 1273 was entrusted to Prior Robert de Estleye for safe keeping (the Prior was in receipt of rents in 1279 for the house of Moses the Jew, who presumably lived in 'Jury' Street before the Jews were expelled in 1290). In 1340, Prior Thomas de Warmington was similarly entrusted with money raised by (Tax) Collectors. The sums of money were quite considerable; in 1293 after collecting a tithe over six years for the Holy Land (the last Crusade was in 1291), the Prior and Convent, as collectors in the Archdeaconries of Coventry and Stafford, accounted for over £1200.

In 1347, Prior John de Peyto lent £16 to the Exchequer in pursuit of the French war, to be repaid by Michaelmas the following year. The Prior also lent £20 to the king for the war in 1379. Private loans were also made: in 1341, 'Sir' Thomas, the Prior, and the Convent lent John, Lord of *Lodbrok* 20 marks, to be repaid the following Easter.

Tax Collector

Edward I (1272-1307) initiated the policy whereby priors were responsible for collecting the clerical and lay taxes for the neighbourhood, although Prior Robert de Estleye was involved in collection as early as 1270. In 1295, Prior Robert de Salle, with the Abbot of Burton on Trent, was the Collector for the diocese of Coventry, and in 1303, the King complained that the Prior of Kenilworth had not collected the 'one tenth' (a 10% tax or tithe) levied on the clergy by Pope Boniface VIII. As Boniface had died, the King claimed the levy was now due to him.

The Prior was assisted in this task to some extent by the canons, as in 1305, John de Leycestre, one of the canons, delivered a roll of taxation to the Exchequer.

Commissioner of the Peace

In 1524, Abbot William was appointed to the Commission of Peace, the only religious superior in the county to receive this honour. This was renewed in 1529, 1532 and 1534. Abbot Simon Jekys was also on the Commission in 1537.

Diocesan visitor

At the General Chapter of the Augustinian Order, at Oseney Abbey in 1439, Prior Thomas Holygreve was appointed Visitor of the diocese of Coventry & Lichfield, and also of St Asaph, Denbighshire. There were problems in visiting St Asaph because *the people there and their language were almost unknown to the visitor, and there seemed no safe way of approach.*

Host

An important part of the prior's duties lay in providing hospitality. During the siege of Kenilworth Castle in 1266, the besieging king, Henry III, was in Kenilworth continuously from 22 July to 15 December, conducting not only the siege, but normal state business as well. Did he do this from a tent outside the Castle, or from the relative comfort of the Priory? For the services and supplies provided to him, the King granted the Priory immunity from further drains on its resources without his special permission. Hospitality was also provided to Edward II and III, and in 1330, in consideration of the Priory's losses through their frequent visits, concessions were granted when the priorship was vacant (*see* Chapter III).

Judge

Prior Robert acted as Papal Judge Delegate in 1175 in a Darley Abbey dispute. In 1177 he was included amongst the judges in a dispute, held before Henry II, between the Abbeys of Gloucester and Reading, and in 1178/9 in a dispute involving Cirencester Abbey; in 1188 he was Papal Judge Delegate in disputes concerning Harrold Priory and also Oseney. In 1206, under a Bull of Innocent III, the Prior of Kenilworth was one of three Judge Delegates to hear a case brought by Luffield Priory.

Call to Parliament

The only recorded call to Parliament was when the Prior of *Kenelworth* was summoned to the famous Parliament of 20 January, 1265, by a reluctant king. When Kenilworth was raised to Abbey status, the Abbot did not join the 25 *mitred* abbots that had gained baronial status and the right to be summoned to Parliament. Not all mitred abbots had, or indeed, coveted this right; the mitred Augustinian Abbots of Cirencester and Waltham attended Parliament, but those of Bristol and Oseney did not.

President of the Augustinian Chapter

In 1288, Prior Richard de Tyvelesford was joint President of the Chapter of the Order of St Augustine – the comment on his performance was that he *ordained nothing, only enjoyning that the ancient rules be observed.* Prior Thomas de Warmington was joint president in 1333. Thomas had also been a Definitor of the Chapter in 1325. The four Definitors were the most powerful men in the Order as they elected the presidents and framed the statutes to be agreed.

——————— † ———————

The records show other occasional activities. In about 1216, Prior William de Barton served on a Papal Commission inquiring into activities of the Abbey of Préaux. In 1313 Prior Thomas de Warmington acted as Godfather to young Thomas Beauchamp, heir to the Earl of Warwick. In 1343, the Pope interceded on behalf of three *poor wretched and afflicted clerks and priests*, Robert Hailkis of Wolricheston, William, son of Henry le Masan, and Robert Spenser of Uttoxeter, asking the Prior to find them livings. In 1380, during John of Gaunt's works at the Castle, the Prior Henry de Bradweye was the supervisor and controller of all payment and expenses for the work. In 1533, Abbot William presided at an inquiry at Warwick, receiving depositions on alleged heresy.

The prior may well have had to travel on occasions to the Papal Court at Rome. In 1273, for instance, Edward I acknowledged that Prior Robert de Estleye was *going beyond the sea*, and he gave Power of Attorney to two of the canons. Whether Robert actually went and for what purpose are not known.

From the foregoing, it is evident that the Superior needed to be a man of some standing. Not all came up to the high level required; Walter was deposed for his 'excesses' in 1208, but this may have been trumped up in the Crown's interest in getting its hands on the Priory; John de Peyto, as already mentioned, died in 1361 after complaints about the Priory had reached the King's ears. It is clear from various sources that superiors in general were not unknown to use their position for personal gain, and they were exhorted not to provide benefit for their families and friends from the convent's resources (and Abbot Pype of Stoneleigh was notorious for this). However, if any canon wished to make an accusation against him, he had firstly to agree to worthy punishment if he failed to make his case. In the main, however, they appear to have been responsible men, 'the good being interred with their bones' (Julius Caesar III.ii).

Whilst there is no evidence that the Priors and Abbots of Kenilworth rose to higher ecclesiastical ranks, Henry Dean, the Augustinian Prior of Llanthony became bishop of Bangor, then of Salisbury, and finally Archbishop of Canterbury in 1501.

VII   THE CONVENT'S ECONOMY

Whether .... the Prior manages the church,
monastery and manors in a competent manner.

Matters to be investigated by a visiting prelate.
The Constitutions of Pope Benedict (1395 - 1404)

The canons' prime duties were spiritual. Food, clothing and all that was necessary for their existence and calling had to be given or purchased. Hospitality had to be provided, and its burden could ruin a house. John of Gaunt, who held Kenilworth Castle, had a large room at the Priory, perhaps surprisingly, and he also instructed that trees be cut down to make *a floor for dancing on at Christmas in the great room of the Priory,* probably because the Great Hall of the Castle was being extensively altered at the time. This 'great room' may have been the refectory, or an area over the Cellarer's Range, or a so-far-unidentified hall in which entertainment was provided for gentry staying at the Priory.

Apart from the day to day expenses, there was building work and maintenance to be paid for, and not just for the Priory, but some of their churches, as mentioned in the last chapter. The general evidence is against the canons doing their own building and maintenance, although some lesser works might have been executed by lay-brethren.

The King demanded loans and grants from time to time, such as in 1332, when Edward III sent clerks to several hundred bishops and religious houses, including Kenilworth, to collect 'answers' to his request for a subsidy to cover the marriage of Eleanor, his sister, to Reginald, the Count of Guilders. Earlier, in about 1310, a tithe had been imposed for the repulsion from England of the Scots under Robert Bruce. It seems the Prior of Kenilworth was able to prove that he had paid the £8 due for his holdings in the Worcestershire diocese (that is, south of the Avon), but a certain Master Robert de Sutton who had been appointed by the Archbishop of Canterbury to collect this, had failed to hand it over. The Archbishop wrote to the Prior of Worcester, in whose custody the money was presumably to be placed, demanding that Master Robert be compelled to yield it, if necessary, by ecclesiastical censure (if Master Sutton had been in Holy Orders, he could have been deposed from these or from office; alternatives were excommunication or public penance). As in so many cases, historical record does not give the sequel.

To provide a regular income, the Priory had been well endowed, particularly on foundation. This income was identified as coming from two sources – *spiritualities,* income deriving from their churches – and *temporalities,* revenues from their manors, lands, dwellings, etc. The difference was important as whilst the priorship was vacant, the king, as patron, claimed the temporalities, which represented (in 1291) more than half the income.

Gifts of churches, land, dwellings and mills continued after foundation, but they fell off sharply when Edward I introduced the Act of Mortmain in 1279; this forbade grants of land to a religious body without royal licence. 'Benefactors' had been giving their estates to religious houses, which were exempt from many of the secular services associated with land tenure (for example, military service), then, by arrangement, retaining them, thus avoiding the service. The Act aimed at preventing this and other malpractices. As a result, licence was needed; it was given when the Priory acquired property at Hughenden in 1285. However, at an Inquisition in 1367, the canons were found to have acquired the manor of Radford Semele without licence; in this case they did not forfeit the property, contrary to custom. When they purchased the manors of Weston *c* 1428 and Wolston *c* 1431 without royal licence, both manors were seized by the king. Even Thomas, earl of Lancaster, had to obtain licence in Mortmain in 1308 when he gave the canons 15 acres of his wood in Kenilworth, called the Fryth, in exchange for their taking a daily load of brushwood.

The Priory needed to have its possessions frequently verified from an independent repository of documents (rather like the Land Registry), not only to detect forgeries, but as a reminder and deterrent to would-be claimants. This verification or *Inspeximus,* was carried out, it seems, whenever a new Archbishop of Canterbury was appointed, for there are *Inspeximi extant* by Theobald (1139-62) and Richard of Dover (1174-85). They were also carried out by popes; the *Inspeximus* of Clement III (1187-91) starts: *Notification by Pope Clement III to Prior Robert of Kenilworth that, following the examples of Popes Honorius II, Innocent II, Eugenius II, Adrian VI and Alexander III, he has confirmed the following possessions of the canons of Kenilworth....* If the provision of such charters was widespread, the Vatican *Scriptorium* must have been kept very busy. The King also confirmed the canons' charters; there are *Inspeximi* and confirmations of Henry I's charter by King Stephen (1136-9) and by Edward II in 1314, when a charge of 5 marks (£3-13-4) was made, such charges being quite usual.

SPIRITUALITIES

These were the income derived from the canons' churches based on one of two levels of church patronage – *either Patroni Ecclesiae* or *Patroni Vicarii.*

During the period leading up to 12th century, considerable changes had been initiated regarding the status of patron and the priest of the parish church.

The patron had usually been a lay *seigneur*, but it became the aim of Urban II (1088-1099) to wrest this authority from him, and to have the parish priest appointed by, and made responsible to, the bishop. At first, churches remained in the domain of the lay *seigneur*, but he had to present his nominated priest to the bishop for approval. This act of presentation was the right of *advowson*. The next stage was for the *seigneur* to transfer the advowson, by gift and for spiritual benefit, to a religious body – such as the priory – which now always nominated and presented the priests to the bishop for appointment. In return for this service, the priest, who was termed the *rector*, received the *rectorial* tithes, or *rectory*, but had to make an annual payment, or *pension*, to the canons in return for having been nominated. In the case of Tanworth church, the advowson was transferred from the canons to Maxstoke Priory, but the canons, in return, received a pension of 2 marks and a stone of wax from the rector.

By a further process, that of 'appropriation', the priory (or any other religious body) could became the rector, effectively owning the church. The parish priest was now called the vicar (the words 'vicar' and 'rector' are derived from the Latin for a substitute and controller, respectively) as before, the vicar was nominated and presented to the bishop by the priory, which now became the *Patronus Vicarius*, and had temporal responsibility for the incumbent. The vicar received the *lesser tithes*, the *vicarial tithes*, or *vicarage*, and the canons received the *rectory*. Permission to appropriate a church was variously given, sometimes by the Bishop, other times by the Pope; Alexander III (1159-81) granted the Priory the appropriation of the churches of Salford Priors, Ettington, Brailes, Wellesbourne, Harbury and Stoneleigh, specifying that the *rectory* was to be used for the provision of the poor and the upkeep of hospitality. But there was clearly misuse of the system; in 1261, Pope Alexander IV warned the bishop of Coventry and Lichfield, amongst many others, against some religious houses claiming all the revenues for themselves. The actual division between the vicarage and the rectory was generally such that the rector received the corn, beans, peas, hay and wood, the vicar receiving the root crops, fruit, meat, milk and cheese; this rule was not hard and fast, and in 1348 the bishop of Worcester had to arbitrate on the division of tithes between the canons and the vicar of Wellesbourne. One form of misuse was for the religious house to appoint *annual vicars*, which allowed the church to lie vacant regularly whilst a new vicar was appointed, the patron taking all the tithes in the interim. Pope Alexander III intervened, however, making it known that he had a preference for *perpetual vicars*.

Details of the churches in the control of the canons are given in the next chapter. Dugdale[14] usefully records the patronage of Warwickshire churches, and lists many of the incumbents. He, incidentally, recorded the appointment of Aymer de Valence to the church of Fenny Compton by the canons, who held the advowson for a time. Aymer was the detestable and avaricious half-brother of Henry III, who acquired a number of livings, and whom the King forced onto the see of Winchester.

In addition to the direct income from churches, there were various grants and bequests, such as for masses to be said for the donor and his family. In 1511, Henry VIII granted the Abbey *licence in Mortmain* to acquire land up to the value of £40 a year in return for a mass in the Name of Jesus every Friday (except Good Friday), for the good estate of the King and his wife Katherine (of Aragon), and for their souls after death. Burial in the Priory was much sought after; a late 12th century charter by Henry de Clinton's cousin, Juliana de St Remy (a de Semilly by birth), granted all her land in Mollington in exchange for the canons receiving her body for burial, should she die in England. Early in King John's reign, Robert, son of Odonis, gave the canons two acres of land in Harbury in return for a mass being said for him every Saturday. In 1209, Cecily, wife of Richard de Barford, gave all her lands in Tysoe in return for prayers for the soul of her son and heir Roger and the burial of her body. Godwin de Wootton in *c* 1216 gave the canons an annual rent of 5s. together with his body which *he determined to be buryed in that monastery*.

There was income to be gained from Pope Nicholas IV's grant in 1290 of *a year and 40 days enjoined penance* (an indulgence) *to all those visiting the church of the monastery of Kenilworth on the feasts of the Blessed Virgin and of St Augustine in whose honour it had been built*. This, incidentally, is the only example found so far of where St Augustine has been directly associated with the Priory. Holy relics in a monastery or church were an incentive for visitors (an arm, claimed to have been St Augustine's, was held by Coventry Priory). What relics Kenilworth held is not known.

TEMPORALITIES

The two main sources of this income were the manors over which the canons had lordship, and miscellaneous lands and dwellings granted to them at various times. Walsgrove's analysis[42] of the Hundred Roll survey of 1279 has shown that the Priory estate in Kenilworth comprised 129 tenancies. The temporalities are dealt with in more detail in the next chapter.

By the time of the Dissolution, the canons had farmed out, that is, let out for rent, all its properties, even the demesne lands which were reserved for their own use. They also sold their rights to the rectorial tithes for an annual cash payment. This step would have eased the management problem, of course, but ultimately led to the capitalism that has been laid at the door of Protestantism.

Geoffrey de Clinton and his son had granted the canons a tithe of all goods coming into the Castle, the pasturing of their cattle in his fields, and the feeding of their pigs in his woodland. But this probably only barely outlasted the de Clintons, as Henry III instructed the Constable of the Castle to remove all animals that were not the King's from the Castle Park, to make way for his own bulls for fattening. The canons were also licensed to fish, with one boat and nets, in the Castle Mere on Thursdays, but it would not have been long before the canons had their own ponds along the line of Finham Brook. Fish were a very important commodity, and the Mere at Kenilworth Castle supplied the King with fish; in 1232, the Governor was instructed to send a quantity of bream to Worcester for Henry III's use at Christmas. Kenilworth was, as we have said, famous for its bream, a fish of *grat esteem and price in antient times.*

Corrodians were 'paying guests', making usually a lump sum payment for hospitality for life. The king, as patron, however, had the right to place his retired retainers in the house without cost to himself. In 1317, Alice, whose husband had served Edward II well in Scotland where he died in service, was sent to Kenilworth Priory to receive maintenance as a free servant. Henry VI gave a corrody at the Priory to John Bryggewater, of the king's chamber, and William Udale, *one of the king's spicery.* The upkeep of these retainers, if long-lived, would have been a drain on the canons' resources.

A small income was derived from the canons' Court Leets, discussed in more detail in Chapter VIII.

Of Warwickshire houses, Kenilworth had the second highest income at the time of Dissolution, the top five being:

Coventry Priory, Benedictine	£808 4s 0d
Kenilworth, Augustinian	£533 15s 4d
Merevale, Cistercian	£254 1s 8d
Nuneaton, Benedictine Nuns	£253 14s 5½d
Stoneleigh, Cistercian	£151 3s 1½d

The breakdown of revenues is to be found in the
Bailiffs' Accounts [3]
and in Monasticon Anglicanum [15]

Despite all this apparent wealth, the canons fell on bad times, notably in 1266 when the army of Simon de Montfort, who was killed at Evesham in 1265, was besieged at Kenilworth Castle by Henry III. The Prior was required to supply the King with 300 quarters of corn *'and other things'* and, in the following year, the King wrote to all the Priory's tenants, asking them to make a contribution to the Priory *in such a manner as they would expect God to bless them.* Stoneleigh Abbey suffered also; soldiers billeted in their grange at Cryfield managed, through negligence, to burn it down. By way of restitution, the King merely confirmed their charters, no doubt foregoing the usual charge.

The aftermath of the Black Death, which struck both in 1349 and 1361, could not have been easy, although there is little that can be directly gleaned for Kenilworth (except that the canons had to replace three priests at nearby St Nicholas' church, incorrectly identified as priors by the VCH). The parish clergy of Warwickshire were generally badly hit (*see* Fig 5), and whilst the Prior of Kenilworth, John de Peyto, survived the first pestilence, he may have succumbed to the second, as he died in 1361. Between a quarter and a half of the population perished, and as a result, the revenues (as of Coventry Priory, for instance) were significantly reduced.

As we have said, by the time of the Dissolution, the Abbey had rented off all its assets for cash, except for the tithes from Wellesbourne, and pasture at Rudfyn, where the Abbey's cattle were kept. The income from its assets, variously assessed as £668.14s.1d (1540) and £557.14s.9½d (1547) was made up approximately from:

	%	
Rent from Rectories	30	
Pension from Rectories	5	
TOTAL SPIRITUALITIES		35
Tenants	22	
Manors	20	
Land	15	
Demesne lands	5	
Mills	1.5	
Proceeds from Courts Leet	1.5	
TOTAL TEMPORALITIES		65
		100

HISTOGRAM OF ANNUAL CLERICAL
APPOINTMENTS BETWEEN 1300 & 1370

KNIGHTLOW HUNDRED, WARWICKSHIRE

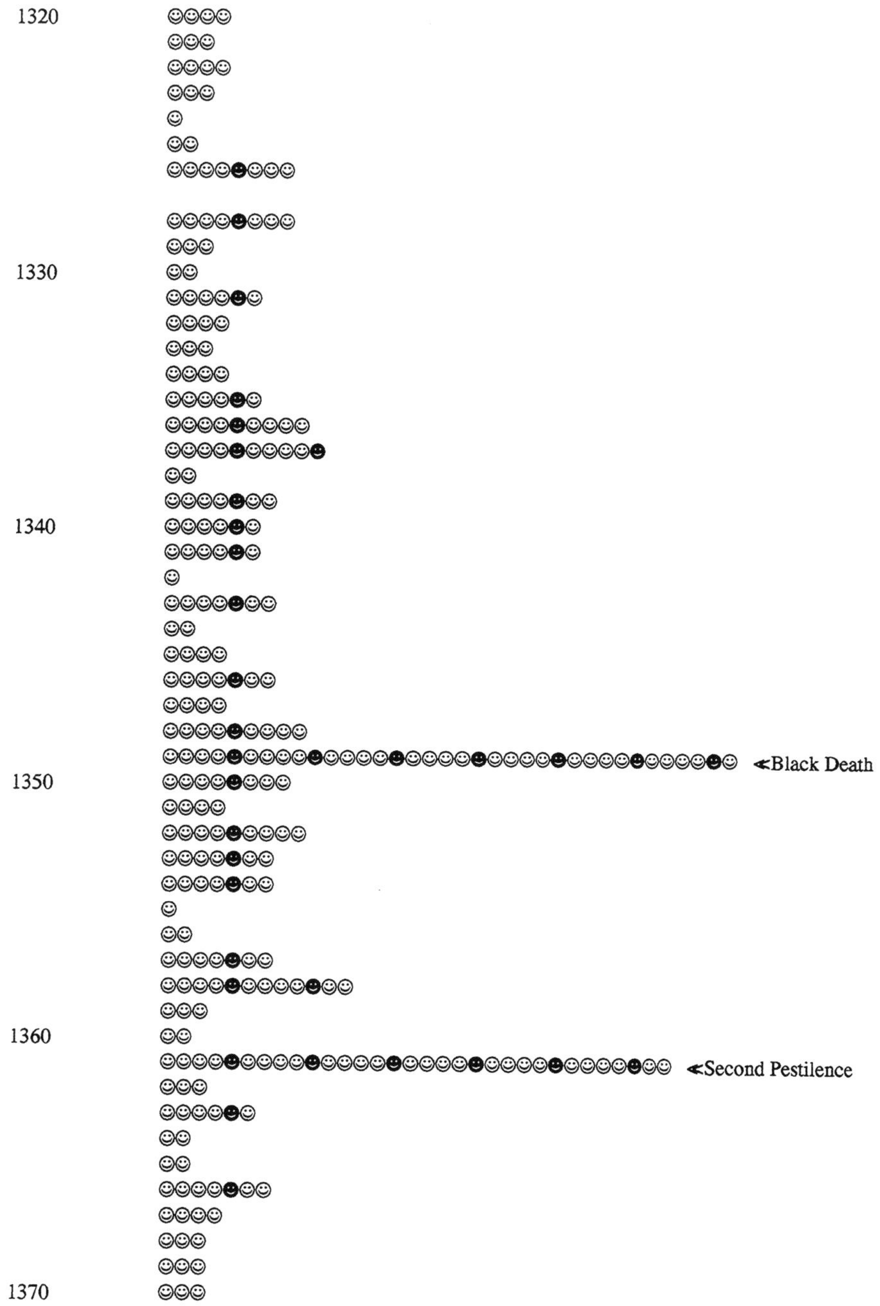

Extracted from 'Mediæval Crockfords' [34]

FIG 5

VIII   THE CANONS' PROPERTIES

..and if my heir is tempted to diminish anything I have granted,
..then let him .... incur a paternal curse and the wrath of God.

Part of Geoffrey de Clinton's Foundation Charter

The canons' properties were considerable and widely spread, as can be seen from Fig. 6. Kenilworth and Coombe Abbey were the third biggest landowners in Warwickshire, only Coventry Priory and the Earl of Warwick holding more.

In the previous chapter, the distinction was made between spiritualities and temporalities, and between appropriated churches (with vicars) and those (with rectors) of which the canons only held the *advowson*. The Table at the end of this chapter itemises 95 locations where the canons had possessions under various headings. To detail all these would require a volume in itself, but a few of the locations have been chosen to indicate the scope of their tenure.

APPROPRIATED CHURCHES

The canons held nineteen appropriated churches in Warwickshire, one in Somerset and two in Buckinghamshire. The reason for the appropriation of the church at Charlton Kanvyle, in Somerset, is not easily explained, but in 1436, the Receiver there, William Sampford, was identified in the Patent Rolls for failing to appear before the bench to answer for his receivership to the Prior of Kenilworth.

'ADVOWSON' CHURCHES

The right to appoint and present the rector to the bishop was held for 21 churches in Warwickshire, two in Derby, one each in Devon and Northampton, and five each in Oxfordshire and Staffordshire, a total of 36. This right was held for only a short time, such as at Tanworth, Fenny Compton and Iffley, but when the advowson was transferred, a pension was received in return.

An analysis of 152 Warwickshire churches detailed in Dugdale (not an exhaustive list) indicates that religious houses and cathedrals held the patronage of approximately two thirds; the remainder were held mainly by the the lords of the manor. Of the first group, two thirds were held by appropriation, the advowson only being held for the remainder. The analysis also shows clearly that Kenilworth held by far the greatest number of Warwickshire churches; after Kenilworth came Coventry Priory, Maxstoke and the Bishop of Worcester, all trailing far behind with only a handful each.

MANORS

The manor was a self-sufficient community of tenant farmers and villeins *(servi)*. The lords had their own land in *demesne* which was worked by some of the tenants. The lord also held his own court, the Court Leet, certain tenants acting as juries, and also deciding communal plans for the manor.

The Kenilworth canons held 14 manors in Warwickshire, and one each in Buckinghamshire, Rutland and Staffordshire.

The Prior held the lordship of half of Kenilworth, the other half being held by whoever held the Castle at the time (roughly half the villages in Warwickshire were held by more than one lord). The Hundred Roll entries for Kenilworth tell that the Prior held his part of Kenilworth as tenant-in-chief from the king; he had 700 acres of land at 'Wridfen' (Rudfyn) and Blackwell (to the west of Kenilworth), he had a water-mill in his lordship, and 23 villeins in his service. Elsewhere, it tells of the Prior having a 28-acre wood, a 'view of frankpledge' (a sort of Neighbourhood Watch scheme, the 'view' being the hearing of cases against law-breakers), the right to use gallows and to hold assizes where the price of bread and beer were fixed. All his tenants are named, with their holdings. He was the landlord of 64 *messuages* (dwellings, with land assigned to their use), 49 cottages and some 100 acres farmed out. Most of the tenants had to give so many days, usually 8 in the year, in the lord's service. This service varied, but included mowing and making hay, reaping corn, carting produce to the Priory, weeding and hoeing and collecting nuts; in one case, a head of cloves, and in another, a pound of wax, had to be provided. Other of the tenants had to give service, usually 2 days a year at the Prior's court (*sectam* and *adventus*), amounting to some 50 man-days in the year. In addition, most had to pay a rent varying from a pepper-corn of ½d, to an average of 1s to 1s 6d. One cottage was leased at 15s a year (a copying error?). Some of the tenancies were 'free', others at the will of the Prior, and some for the life of the tenant, others allowing it to pass down to one heir. As Walsgrove[42] points out, the names of the tenants suggest urban activities – Turner, Ropere, Pypere, Tayleresse, Taylor, Ferur, Palmer, Porter, Mercer, Carpenter, Lactere, and so on, their trades no doubt being centred on the Priory and Castle.

The Bailiffs' Accounts[3] of 1547 for Kenilworth are of interest as they give names of localities – Glynton Grene, Shooters Close, High Street, &c. Walsgrove[43] has analysed the Abbey lands here, showing that High Street was owned by the Abbey, and suggesting that four properties had probably been occupied by lay people in the employ of the Abbey.

The Roll also shows that the Prior was the sole lord of Leamington, but unlike Kenilworth, he did not hold it directly from the king, but from Gilbert de Norton, who held it from the Prior of Coventry, who held it from the king – a fairly typical feudal chain. He held one water mill and about 100 acres in demesne, as well as a share of another water mill. As at most of his manors, the Prior had the right to hang thieves, and hold Assizes of Bread and Ale. The service conditions were generally similar to Kenilworth except for the frequent addition that they had to provide the Prior with hens and cockerels at Christmas time.

TOWNS

The influence of the Prior on the local, and not so local, communities, is seen in a Chartered Roll (a royal charter) of 1459. In this, Henry VI, *out of consideration for the burdens of the Abbot and Convent of St Mary Kenilworth, and out of special grace to John Yardley the Abbot, and his successors,* granted the *Abbot's bailiff of the town of Kenilworth,* the same rights as the king's steward, marshall and coroner, within a number of 'towns'. These are listed in the appendix to this chapter, and include a number that were not listed as manors. Furthermore, the Abbot's bailiff and other officers had precedence over the king's officers in these towns and manors. The Abbot had claim on the chattels of convicted felons, fugitives, outlaws and suicides within these places, and the "fines" (fees) for all transactions that normally carry them. The Abbey seems to have gained impressive immunity from interference in its manors, and elsewhere. No similar charter for other Warwickshire houses has been noted for the period except one to St Mary's Priory, Coventry, granting them the rights on the chattels of convicted felons, &c. The fact that this charter was issued by Henry VI is further indication of benign involvement with the monastery at Kenilworth (*see* Chapter XI, the Raising to Abbey Status).

OTHER HOLDINGS

Kenilworth had a variety of other holdings – messuages, cottages, crofts, land, meadows and mills. The table below gives the number of Warwickshire tenancies held by the Prior in 1280, including those in his manors.

Kenilworth	129	
Leamington	30	
Lillington	28	
Tysoe	25	(including Westcote in Tysoe)
Harbury	22	
Idlicote	19	
Stoneleigh	16	
Ashow	14	
Leek Wootton	14	(including Hill Wootton)
Radford Semele	14	
Warwick	5	(town houses)
Mollington	8	
Baginton	6	
Halford	4	
Kineton	4	
	338	

Included in these are the mill at Guy's Cliff, granted to the canons by Geoffrey II, the son of the founder; he also granted the canons whatever rights may belong to him in respect of the mill, the miller, and the miller's children. The Prior also held in lordship a windmill and 60 acres of land in Harbury.

Not included in the above are certain properties acquired later in Coventry: the Augmentation Office shows rents to the value of £7 14s 10d from Coventry. In 1359, or earlier, the Black Prince took steps to release property in Coventry, with licence in Mortmain, to the Prior and Convent of Kenilworth. Nothing had happened by April, 1359, so the Prior and John le Porter, who held the land in question from the Prince, petitioned him so that the matter might proceed. The Prince then ordered the Mayor of Coventry to set up an inquisition to determine in depth the consequences, both to the Prince and John le Porter's standing in Coventry, were the matter to proceed – John might have lost his rights to serve on juries, &c, if he no longer held land there. By now, the properties had been identified as a cottage in 'Le Brodeyate', 2 shops and a cottage in 'Le West-orchard', 2 shops and a cottage in 'Hullestret', a cottage in 'Wellestret, and a cottage at 'Smethford-brugge'. It would seem that this transaction was not effected, however, probably due to the death of John le Porter, for, when it surfaced again in May, 1364, licence was sought for John le Porter the Younger, for the *weal* of his soul, to assign to the Prior and Convent an alternative group of properties: a messuage in 'Brodeyate', a messuage in 'Wellestret', a messuage each in 'Wellestret' and 'Hillestret', a yearly rent of 6s 6d from a bridge of Smytheford, a messuage in 'Erlestrete' at 'Mullanende' and the reversion of a messuage in 'Litelparkstret' in 'Mullanende' expected on the demise of the widow holding it. The conclusion of this matter is not recorded, but it is likely that these were the properties held by the Priory. John le Porter (or John le Potter) seems to have been an influential man who had permission from the bishop to have his own oratory in Kenilworth.

A full analysis of the canons' holdings has yet to be attempted, but if ever completed, it will make fascinating reading. It will already be appreciated that there would have been a considerable administrative effort to control the Priory's assets, until its latter days when practically all were farmed out.

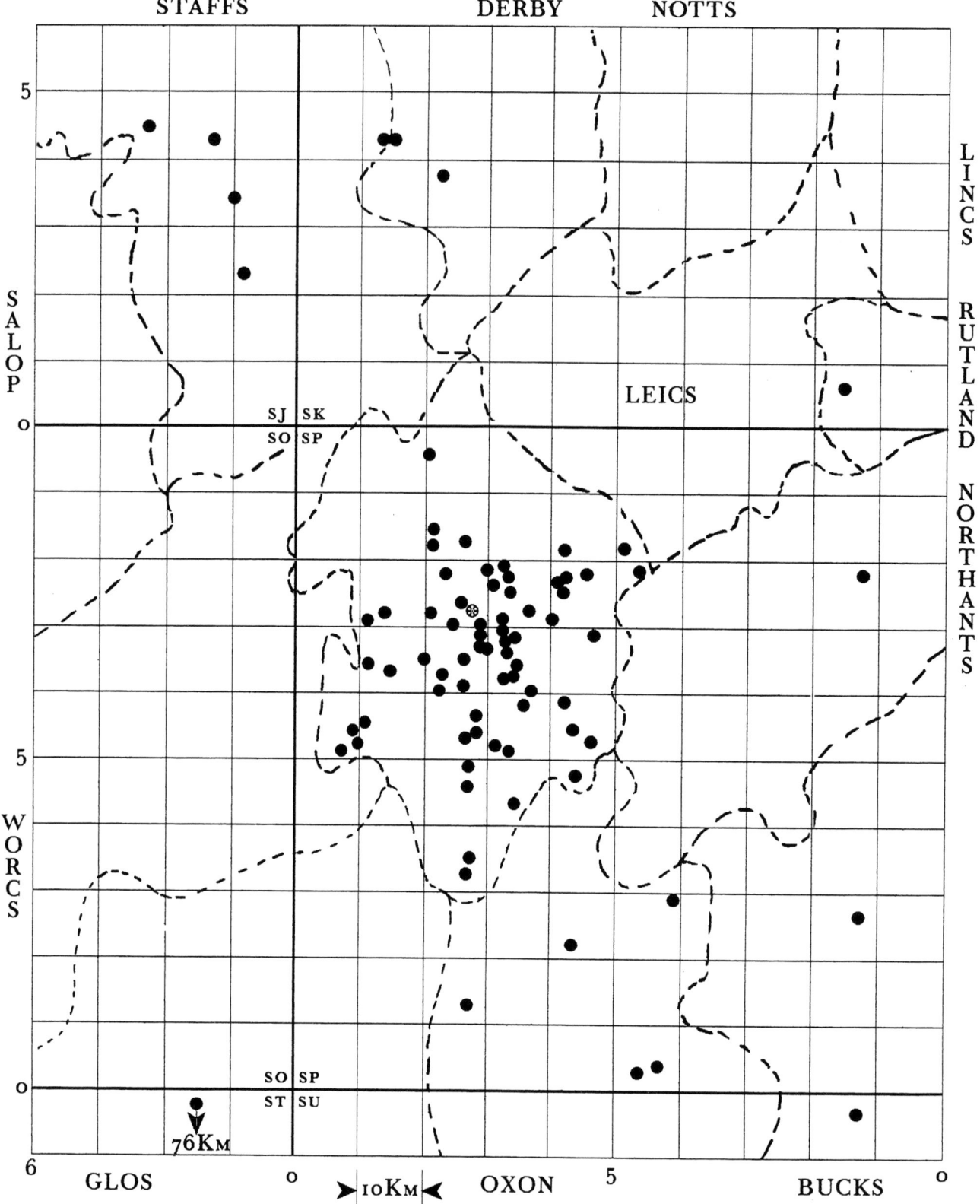

LOCATIONS OF SITES HELD BY THE CANONS OF KENILWORTH

See Appendix to Chapter VIII for details

(KENILWORTH IS MARKED ⊕)

FIG 6

HS 1994

TABLE HEADINGS

Cells: these are dealt with in Chapter X, but are included for completeness.

App: churches that are appropriated (*Patroni Vicarii*)

Adv: churches for which the canons have advowson only (*Patroni Ecclesiae*)

Man: manors for which the Prior is lord, although often shared with other lords. Where there is evidence of the Abbey having obtained revenue from a court (leet), it is assumed that manorial rights were held.

Town: places mentioned in the Chartered Roll of 1459, whereby extensive rights were granted.

Other: this covers a variety of holdings – a few acres of land, meadows, mills, cottages, messuages, crofts and town houses, far too varied to list here, the aim being to show the geographical extent of the holdings, rather than content.

Map: In many cases, these map references are approximate, as the exact location of the feature may not be known. In these cases, the reference has centred on the village, town etc. A few, as indicated, are uncertain, and some have not yet been identified.

As a general note, it should be recognised that not all the possessions were held over the major period of the Priory/Abbey's existence, but a majority were.

Sources: each location is given only one reference, usually the earliest, although it may appear in others.

A = Foundation Charter and Harley 3650
B = Hundred Rolls of 1279-80
C = Close Rolls, E.II
D = Chartered Roll of 1459
E = Abstract of Roll 31, Hen.VIII, in *Monasticon.*
F = Bailiffs' Accounts of 1547
G = *Antiquities of Warwickshire*, William Dugdale, 1656
O = Other

| | | SPIRITUALITIES | | TEMPORALITIES | | | | |
	LOCATION	Cell	App	Adv	Man	Town	Other	Map
	WARWICKSHIRE							
1	Allesley	.	.	.	.	.	A	SP 262 817
2	Ashow	.	.	A	.	D	A	SP 312 702
3	Baddesley Clinton	.	.	G	.	.	.	SP 203 713
4	Baginton	.	.	A	.	.	A	SP 343 747
5	Balsall Common	.	.	.	.	.	E	SP 238 770
6	Barford	.	.	.	.	.	E	SP 268 607
7	Barton-on-the-Heath	.	.	.	.	.	A	SP 257 327
8	Bidford	.	A	.	.	.	.	SP 100 520
9	Bishops Tachbrook	.	.	.	.	D	A	SP 313 611
10	Brailes	.	G	.	.	D	B	SP 313 393
11	Blackwell	.	.	.	.	.	A	SP 255 733
12	Brandon	.	.	.	.	.	A	SP 408 765
13	Bretford	.	.	.	.	.	B	SP 428 772
14	Brinklow	.	.	A	.	.	.	SP 437 797
15	Bubbenhall	.	.	.	.	.	E	SP 362 723
16	Canley	.	.	.	.	.	E	SP 305 764
17	Chesterton	.	.	A	.	.	.	SP 358 582
18	Churchover	.	.	.	.	.	E	SP 509 808
19	Claverdon	.	.	A	.	.	.	SP 200 651
20	Combrook	.	.	?	.	.	.	SP 305 517
21	Coventry	.	.	.	.	.	E	SP 329 791
22	Cruce	.	.	.	.	D	.	SP 291 700?
23	Cubbington	.	A	.	.	.	.	SP 344 683
24	Ettington	.	A	.	.	D	.	SP 267 490
25	Exhall	.	.	A	.	.	.	SP 105 550
26	Fenny Compton	.	.	A	.	.	A	SP 417 521
27	Fletchampstead	.	.	.	.	.	E	SP 300 780?
28	Guy's Cliffe	.	.	.	.	.	A	SP 290 670
29	Halford	.	.	E	.	D	A	SP 261 453

	LOCATION	SPIRITUALITIES		TEMPORALITIES				Map
		Cell	App	Adv	Man	Town	Other	
	WARWICKSHIRE (contd)							
30	Hampton-in-Arden	.	.	E	.	.	.	SP 203 808
31	Harbury	.	A	.	B	D	A	SP 374 600
32	Hodnell	.	.	A	.	.	.	?
33	Idlicote	.	.	.	A	.	.	SP 282 442
4	Kenilworth	.	G	.	A	.	A	SP 286 724
35	Kineton	.	A	.	.	D	A	SP 335 510
36	King's Newnham	.	A	.	A	.	.	SP 452 773
37	Kite's Hardwick	.	.	.	.	.	A	SP 470 680
38	Ladbroke	.	.	.	.	.	A	SP 415 589
39	Lamcote	.	.	.	.	D	E	?
40	Leamington	.	A	.	A	.	.	SP 320 654
41	Leek Wootton	.	A	.	B	.	A	SP 289 688
42	Lillington	.	A	.	B	D	A	SP 333 672
43	Loxley	.	A	.	E	.	.	SP 259 530
44	Marston	.	.	.	.	.	F	SP 200 955
45	Milverton	.	A	.	.	.	.	SP 297 674
46	Morton Bagot	.	.	G	.	.	.	SP 113 647
47	Newton	.	.	.	.	D	A	SP 530 782
48	Norton Lindsey	.	.	.	.	.	E	SP 229 632
49	Nuthurst	.	.	A	.	.	.	SP 146 721
50	Packington	.	G	.	A	D	.	SP 212 842
51	Princethorpe	.	.	.	.	.	E	SP 400 707
52	Radford Semele	.	A	.	B	D	.	SP 345 645
53	Rudfyn	.	.	.	B	.	.	SP 258 738
54	Salford Priors	.	A	.	A	.	.	SP 075 510
55	Smite	.	.	A	.	.	.	SP 412 808?
56	Snitterfield	.	.	A	.	.	.	SP 215 600
57	Stoneleigh	.	A	.	G	D	.	SP 330 726
58	Tanworth	.	.	A	.	.	.	SP 113 706
59	Tysoe	.	.	.	B	D	A	SP 338 438
60	Walton	.	.	A	.	.	.	SP 285 534
61	Warwick	.	.	.	.	.	A	SP 283 650
62	Waver(?)	.	.	.	.	D	.	?
63	Wellesbourne	.	A	.	.	D	.	SP 277 556
64	Whitnash	.	.	A	.	.	.	SP 328 637
65	Wixford	.	.	A	.	.	.	SP 091 545
66	Wolford	.	.	A	.	.	.	SP 260 350
67	Wolston	.	.	.	.	.	G	SP 413 755
68	Wormleighton	.	A	.	.	.	.	SP 448 540
69	Wootton Wawen	.	.	.	.	.	A	SP 148 630
	BUCKINGHAMSHIRE							
70	Hughendon	.	A	.	A	.	.	SU 861 967
71	Stewkley	.	A	.	.	.	.	SP 848 263
	DERBYSHIRE							
72	Longford	.	.	A	.	.	.	SK 219 380
73	Ellastone	.	.	A	.	.	.	SK 115 428
	DEVON (?)							
74	Colyton	.	.	C	.	.	.	SY 251 938
	LEICESTERSHIRE							
75	Oadby	.	.	.	.	.	E	SX 624 004
	NORTHAMPTONSHIRE							
76	Barton Seagrave	.	.	A	.	.	.	SP 886 776
77	Normanton	.	.	.	.	.	A	?
	OXFORDSHIRE							
78	Cowley	.	.	.	.	.	A	SP 553 038
79	Dudwell	.	.	.	.	.	E	?
80	Fulbrook	.	.	.	.	.	E	SP 265 133
81	Glympton	.	.	A	.	.	.	SP 424 218

	LOCATION	SPIRITUALITIES		TEMPORALITIES LOCATION				
		Cell	App	Adv	Man	Town	Other	Map
	OXFORDSHIRE (contd)							
82	Hethe	.	.	A	.	.	.	SP 591 294
83	Iffley	.	.	A	.	.	.	SP 526 035
84	Ludwell	.	.	A	.	.	.	SP 435 223
85	Mollington	.	.	E	.	D	A	SP 442 476
	RUTLAND							
86	Brooke	G	.	.	A	D	.	SK 848 059
	SOMERSET							
87	Charlton Kanvyle	.	A	.	.	.	.	ST 666 238
	STAFFORDSHIRE							
88	Calwich	G	.	E	.	.	.	SK 123 430
89	Madeley	.	.	A	.	.	.	SJ 772 448
90	Milwich	.	O	.	.	.	.	SJ 966 323
91	Patteshull	.	.	.	G	.	.	SJ 802 009
92	Rickerscote	.	.	.	.	.	A	?
93	Stafford (St Nich.)	.	.	A	.	.	.	SJ 911 225
94	Stallington	.	.	.	.	.	A	?
95	Stoke	.	.	A	.	.	.	SJ 870 457
96	Stone	G	.	A	.	.	.	SJ 900 342

IX THE MONASTERY

*It was if the world had cast off its old age, everywhere
investing itself with the white mantle of churches.*

Raoul Glaber, an 11th century monk.

The canons lived, worked and served God in their monastery. Despite three excavations, there is still much to be discovered of the buildings. The main work available is Carey-Hill's report[4] of Crouch's excavation in 1922.

THE SITE

The remains lie on the steep south-facing slope of the Finham Brook valley; High Street lies to the north, known then as *Alta Strada* and, later, as High Town, with houses on each side of the road. A quarry lay just to the north. From High Street, land falls 20 metres (64 ft) to the Brook. Thus the monastery was heavily stepped in the north-south elevation.

Six hundred metres away to the west lies Kenilworth Castle, to outlast the Abbey and continue as a fortress and palace until 1649. Between the Castle and the Abbey was another quarry and masons' yard, later occupied by the seventeenth century cottages of Little Virginia, excavated by the History & Archaeology Society in 1973[38].

Along the line of the Brook, between the Castle and the Abbey lay the Abbey Pool; now known as the Oxpen Meadow, it is usually flooded in the winter for skating, and consideration is being given to its permanency as a lake. A mill is shown on maps as being on the south side of the Brook, opposite the swimming pool, and evidence of buildings of unknown function was exposed in this area in 1990, when the Severn-Trent Water Company laid a pipeline. Water from the mill formed a stream, feeding into Bakehouse Pool, below the Abbey. The stream continued eastwards, as it does today, through School Lane meadow and Odibourne Allotments. There were at least two mills in School Lane Meadow and beyond, but these seem to have been post-Dissolution features. To the south of the Abbey, over the brook, the land rises steeply up the valley to the same height as High Street, with the town, Geoffrey de Clinton's borough, beyond. Figure 7 is a composite map showing the main features of the area.

A Survey[21] made of the Castle some time between 1538 and 1547, tells of the Abbey site containing 20 acres, enclosed by a stone wall. This area approximates to the north side of the Abbey Fields, less the areas of the Abbey pools, and is generally in line with the 1692 map of James Fish. The implication of the Abbey wall extending westerly almost to the Castle is borne out by the investigation at Little Virginia, mentioned above. The foundations of a wall, dated as 12th/13th century from associated pottery, ran through the site towards the Castle, and then turned sharply in a southerly direction, following the Abbey boundary as shown on Fish's Map.

Eleven acres were identified in the Bailiffs' report[3] of 1547, broken down into: *The Great Orchard*, 5 acres; A pasture called the *Sextry*, 1 acre; the *Farmery* (Fermery) *Garden*, with orchard and pool, 1 acre; the *Yonge Orchard and pool* adjacent to the *Bak-House pool*, 3 acres; the *Vynyard*, 1 acre.

There is no surviving plan, but the pasture is likely to have been on the west of the site, where the Fish Map identifies the Abbey Meadow. Whitley's plan[45] shows two pools where the tennis courts are now, and the site of the present bowling green as the site of the mill, granary and farm buildings; the grounds for these assertions are not known. On the other hand, Aston & Bonde[1] give all this area as the Bakehouse Pool. These matters can perhaps be resolved as and when 'non-destructive' archæological survey techniques are applied to the Abbey Fields.

The main entrance was from the *Alta Strata* through the 14th century Gatehouse, the track still visible as a hollow way. This extended to the mill, where the stream was crossed by 'Abbey Bridge'. There is a 1629 entry in the Churchwardens' Accounts, *Item paid for mending the Abbie Bridge beinge the Church-way xx^d*. In 1673, it was washed away by flood and was probably not rebuilt until 1735. By 1890 it had disappeared again, and on Whitley's plan it appears as *Remains of Packhorse Bridge*.

THE ABBEY LAYOUT

Although the Augustinians had more houses than any order in England, their detail within the overall plan was, as might be expected, flexible; the earlier church buildings of the 12th century tended to follow the Benedictine and Cluniac styles, but were later more influenced by the Cistercians.

Figure 8 is a simplified version of the plan of the site excavation of *c* 1923[4]. Due to the intrusion of the Churchyard, some features have not been excavated, but the basic layout is traditional, used by all orders. Most monasteries were built on south-facing slopes to get full benefit of the sun in the cloister.

The essential facilities of Kenilworth were built in the usual way around a central court, the Cloister and its Garth. The cruciform Church was on the north side. The east side was formed by the Chapter House and the *Dorter*, or dormitory, terminating in the *Reredorter*, or latrine. The south held the *Frater*, or refectory, and, if custom were followed, the *Cellarer's Range*, or storage area, was on the west side with, possibly, hospitality facilities above. An artist's impression of the early layout is shown in Figure 9. Outside this 'core' lay the *Fermery* (Infirmary) to the east, and the *Gatehouse* and the *'Barn'* – the supposed Guest House – to the west.

The following chronology of the buildings is based on Carey-Hill's report, for which he consulted Harold Brakspear, an expert on abbeys, and that ubiquitous Warwickshire antiquarian, Philip B Chatwin. Broadly, the development appears as:

12th Century There is no record of any temporary timber buildings that could have housed the first canons. The Church with the Chapter House alongside, and possibly the first part of the Dorter are Norman. The Cloister may also have been constructed at this time, and also the boundary wall.

13th Century The South Range of the Cloister and possibly the unexcavated west range are Early English, as also is the Parlour adjacent to the west end of the Church. The Church itself underwent considerable change in the late 13th Century, the transepts extended and the crossing rebuilt. A new doorway was inserted at the west end of the Nave. The Fermery was probably built at this time.

14th Century The Presbytery at the east end of the church was extended. The Gatehouse and the 'Barn' are also of this period.

15th Century The Dorter was extended southwards. It was in the mid-15th century that the monastery was raised to the status of an Abbey, and this may well have accompanied the erection of 'prestige' buildings yet to be identified – such as an Abbot's House.

THE CHURCH

The Church has a long narrow Nave, long Transepts and a long Presbytery. By Augustinian standards, the length of the church, 86 metres (283 ft), is 25% greater than the average, but shorter than some, including Bristol and Carlisle.

Unusually, the nave had no aisles. The naves of canons' churches were used by the public, but at Kenilworth, the nearby parish church of St Nicholas' had been built by 1291, so there was little incentive to add aisles to the Priory church.

Doorways at each end of the Nave led into the cloister, and formed a part of the processional way used on Sundays and other feast days. At the west end, the original Norman doorway had been replaced by an Early English doorway and outside of this there was some form of enclosure. The nave was clearly in full use in 1340, as 112 deacons and 37 priests were ordained in the church at Kenilworth.

To give an idea of size, the length of the Nave alone equalled the whole length of nearby St Nicholas' Church, and was of similar width, excluding the aisles. In its final form, the whole church was more than twice the length of St Nicholas'. Based on the proportions of similar Augustinian churches, such as Dorchester and Lanercost, the likely height of the walls was 11 metres or 45 feet, a fairly imposing structure.

The original north and south 'arms' or transepts of the church were almost trebled in length for the provision of the chapels, as, in time, every canon became required to say mass daily. This extension, which Carey-Hill placed in the 13th Century, would have required the reconstruction of the original Norman tower above the crossing; as there was a separate bell-tower built about this time, it probably remained low or non-existent, as at Exeter (where the towers are over the transepts).

The Quire, used by the non-officiating canons during services, separated the transepts along the line of the nave. The Presbytery, the area where the officiating priests conducted the services, is 14th century, having been moved west from an earlier position by the extension of the transepts. It is long and aisleless, the main altar being situated at its east end, mounted on a dais having three steps.

Business with outsiders was conducted in the narrow Parlour by the west end of the church. Below the level of the church, there was a further drop of three steps to the cloister.

BELL-TOWER

Today, just to the north of the west end of the Priory church, in the churchyard, there is a quadrilateral pit, variously referred to as the Monks, Monk's or Monks' Hole. Three sides are 19th century retaining walls, the fourth being the massive plinth of one side of an octagon. Although only one side is now exposed, according to 1840 newspaper accounts, four sides had been. The possibility of it being the base of a Bell-tower, as suggested in 1890, has been re-affirmed[37], and it is probably the puzzling west tower of the church, shown on the Priory seal, Figure 10a. It was built in the first half of the 13th century, probably because of problems with the church tower; a 13th Century bell tower was erected at Worcester Abbey (now Cathedral) after the tower fell down in 1175, and there are other precedents.

CLOISTER

The cloister was some 45% larger in area than the average for an Augustinian house. Some 1.2 metres lower than the church, the walk-way was 3m (10ft) wide with seating along the outer wall; Carey-Hill suggests it was rebuilt in the 13th century. Each arm of the square comprised six bays with a lean-to type roof over the walk-way, supported possibly by a stone-shafted arcade.

The Cloister was not just a convenient means of communication between the central buildings, but the northern sunnier side was normally used as an area in which the canons worked. Some cloisters had cubicles called 'carrels' created by screening fitted in between the roof supports and providing some protection in winter.

SLYPE AND FERMERY

The South Transept and the Chapter House were separated by a 3 metre wide passage, the Slype, which was entered up two steps through a Norman doorway; it had stone seats on each wall. This led up two more steps to the Fermery, and also probably the canons' Graveyard, to the east. The Slype also served as the inner parlour where discussions among the officers took place.

The two-storey Fermery beyond comprised mainly a hall and chapel, with a possible kitchen at the south-east corner.

CHAPTER HOUSE

Second to the church in importance, the Chapter House was a Norman building with a rounded end. It was large, 15 metres long and 8·5 metres wide (49½ x 28 ft), slightly larger than its famous counterpart at the Augustinian Abbey of Bristol.

During the 1922 excavation, several separate stone vaulting ribs and voussoirs (wedged arch members) were found on the floor. These are heavily moulded with chevron and other Norman or Romanesque decoration. They were painted, mainly red and white, with some grey/blue, traces of which remain; two have vestiges of painted designs. These are sculpturally similar to those in the Chapter House at Bristol. Curiously, pieces of Romano-British tile were found with the vaulting. These have been identified as having come from the Kenilworth Chase Wood R-B tile kiln but there is no suggestion whatsoever that the Priory site occupied an earlier Roman Villa. Carey-Hill suggests they were used as wedges in the vaulting.

One of the dominant features of the Abbey Fields today is the remains of the Chapter House south wall, standing gauntly in isolation and providing a starting point for young, would-be mountaineers. Its lower part is concealed, but its full height is over 20 ft (6 metres). 2 metres thick, it is of rubble-work with very little coursing. Bucks' engraving of 1729 (Fig 11), a south view (incorrectly entitled *The East View.....*) shows blind arcading with round inter-secting on the inside wall. This also was incorrect, as the remains of a pointed arch were still grimly ad-hering to that wall, until they fell in the winter of 1926/7. That it was an arcade of pointed arches is confirmed by an earlier Buck drawing and suggests completion in the late 12th century.

Although the internal plan of the apse is circular, the external wall was altered in the 13th century to a five-sided polygon above the original semicircular foundation, with shallow buttresses between each side.

There was stone seating around the inside walls. Any floor tiling had been removed, but beneath the rubble there were two stone coffins, said to be those of Geoffrey de Clinton and his son; there is uncertainty on this, as discussed in Chapter XIV.

DORMITORY AND WATER SUPPLY

Built on steeply sloping ground, the original dormitory or *dorter* was, unusually, on the ground floor, in fact two steps down from the cloister. For the 15th century extension, the dorter was on the first floor.

This later extension terminates in the *rere-dorter* or latrine that would have had a constant flow of water, possibly channelled from the Abbey Pool and returned to Finham Brook – and no doubt used by any populace that may have lived downstream, although the latter's drinking water would have come from the Common Lane springs. In any case, the Abbey itself was downstream of the Castle where the water from the Brook would have been similarly polluted, to flow thence via the various fish-ponds to the Abbey. It is said[1] that a certain amount of sewage in fishponds is not harmful as it supports plankton on which fish feed. Too much suppresses the necessary pond bacteria.

However, the canons' clean water supply came from sources in the High Street area, above; in 1251, licence was given to channel water from the well of Edith Lawtherin via a conduit through the court and house of the Priory, provided she was recompensed.

One of the persisting local stories concerns the secret passage from the Abbey to the Castle; there are those who claim to have been part-way along it in their youth. There was a 4 ft wide and 5 ft deep (1·2 x 1·5 metres) early rere-dorter drain running east-west from the old Dorter to the Fermery. This is likely to have initiated the tale.

REFECTORY

The south side of the cloister had, at the east end, the 'Dark Entry', so-called by Carey-Hill from an example at Canterbury. This passage, entered down five steps, led through to a second court where there are probably buildings yet to be located. Next to this was the Refectory or *Frater*, only partially excavated because of the overlying churchyard. A two-storied building, its ground floor was nearly a metre below the adjacent cloister walk. There was plaster on the north and east walls, with a painted fret-pattern, apparently destroyed by exposure before it could be recorded.REMAINDER OF SOUTH RANGE

AND WEST RANGE

The remainder of the the cloister lies below the churchyard. However, the west range usually belonged to the Cellarer because it was conveniently nearer the entrance to the site for the delivery of provisions. The upper floor of the range could be used for housing guests, and it was here, perhaps, that John of Gaunt had his 'large room'.

OUTER COURT

This lay to the west of the above buildings, and contained the two largely extant buildings of the Abbey, the Gatehouse and the 'Barn', both 14th century buildings.

GATEHOUSE

Known locally as the Tantara Gatehouse, it is shown on the Fish Map of 1692 as *Tantarrow*. A story persists that the name is derived from bugle calls from coachmen to attract the attention of the porter: *tan-tar-rah*. The Stoneleigh Estate has an eastern entrance, the Tantara Lodge which appears to be a later imitation of the Kenilworth Gatehouse, and is alleged to have this name from the warning given when Lord Leigh approached.

Most of the surviving monastic Gatehouses, as Kenilworth's, were products of the turbulent 14th Century, when it was necessary to look to defences. Figure 12 shows the Gatehouse. The building conforms to a typical design (Maxstoke, for instance), where the entrance is formed of two bays, separated by a wall pierced with a larger carriage entrance and a smaller pedestrian entrance. Each bay has a recess in the west wall, no doubt with seating for those who waited. To the west is a two-roomed Porter's Lodge, the inner room having an upper floor, with latrines at both levels.

Current study suggests several phases of development, including at one time, a turret for access to a room over the archway, as was usual. The building once extended both to the south and the east, and evidence [24] was found of further buildings on the west and north sides during a minor excavation in 1976. This was in advance of a major £20,000 consolidation by the Kenilworth Abbey Advisory Committee, but for which the Gatehouse would now have collapsed due largely to root damage – it had been covered with ivy and trees were growing from the top.

THE 'BARN'

The two-storied 'Barn' is an enigma: described as a guest-house, an almonry, an Fermery, and a fish-house (because of its superficial similarity to that at Glastonbury), its monastic function is still uncertain. After the Dissolution, it lost its roof and was re-roofed about a century later, when it was used as a barn, and the name has stuck. Like the Gatehouse, with which it shares a rare mason's mark, it is essentially mid-14th century.

Figure 14a shows a view from the south-west. The front south face has a central ground-floor doorway. On the west side there is a scar on the wall where there were steps leading up to the entrance door for the first floor. It will be noted that there is a projecting string-course a little lower than the first-floor windows on the front, now thought by the authors to be associated with a single-pitch, or 'lean-to', roof that ran along most of the front of the building, part of the west side and up over the stairway to provide a covered way between the external doors. The string-course is missing on the east side of the front, beyond the door, and is replaced by four beam-slots, indicating a wing extending southwards. A photograph of the Abbey Fields of *c* 1865 in fact shows such a building (Fig 14b) but it is improbable that this was the original monastic version. Another shows a small barn alongside this extension, almost certainly of later origin.

There are also timber slots around the south door itself, indicative of a porch. This is unexpected, as it would duplicate the function of the projecting roof above. It is likely, therefore, that this was a later addition, perhaps after the roof above fell.

The building interior has features associated with its past uses – too numerous to detail here – and these are still being analysed to produce a coherent explanation of the building's function.

The remaining Abbey sculptures are housed and exhibited in the 'Barn', and the Abbey Advisory Committee as re-instated the first floor for the better display of them.

LEGEND FOR Fig 7

SCHEMATIC LAYOUT OF ABBEY

c 1538

1　St Nicholas' Church, founded pre-1291

2　The present Townpool Bridge

3　The Bailiffs' Accounts refer to a pool of the 'Yonge Orchard' adjacent to the *Bak-house*, both in the *Fernery Garden*. The Fish Map of 1692 shows two pools in this area, as shown

4　Whitley's Plan gives this as the site of granaries and farm buildings. His evidence for this is not known - the area is now under the bowling green and tennis courts

5　Site of Mill. Detail maps of the area have shown a mill, and a cursory examination in January, 1989 confirmed the presence of buildings in this area. There is post-Dissolution evidence for the adjacent Abbey Bridge

6　Whitley's Plan also shows the site of a boathouse here. There is a depression in the bank of the lake at this point, and, although the evidence for his statement is unknown,

7　it is quite credible; in this case, nets and the like would have been stored here

8　The site of the 1841 bridge in Castle Road. To the south, the outline of the Castle Fishponds can be seen

9　Site of the present ford. There was probably a causeway and/or bridge spanning this area

10　During the 1973 excavation of the Little Virginia area, a 12/13th century wall was exposed, turning in a southerly direction. This is almost certainly the Abbey boundary wall

11　In the above excavation, Little Virginia was found to be the site of quarrying and a masons' yard, prior to the present dwellings of the first half of the seventeenth century

NOTE: The field names shown are from the 1692 map of James Fish, and may not have applied in monastic times

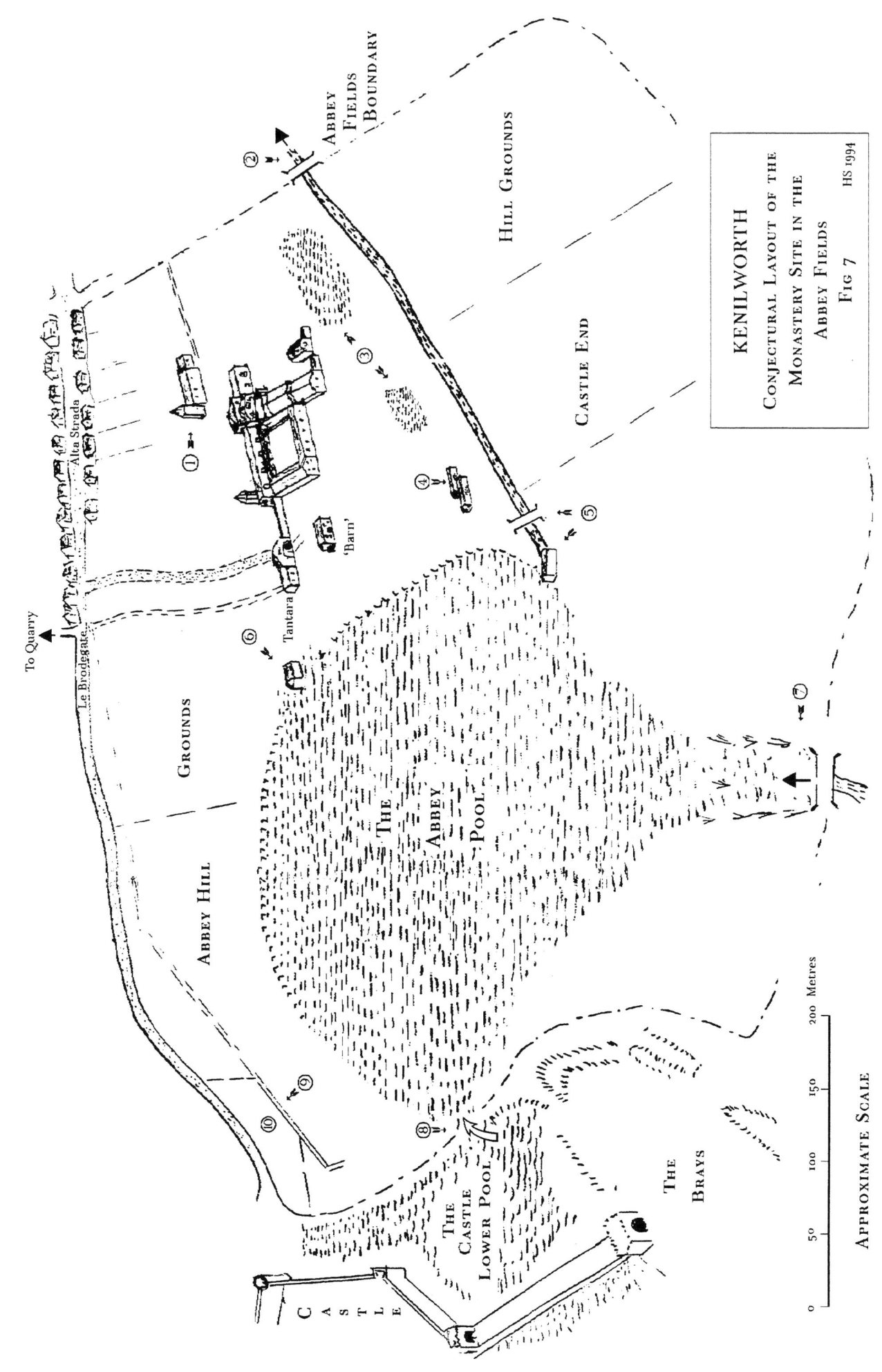

KENILWORTH

CONJECTURAL LAYOUT OF THE
MONASTERY SITE IN THE
ABBEY FIELDS

FIG 7   HS 1994

ABBEY FIELDS BOUNDARY

HILL GROUNDS

CASTLE END

THE ABBEY POOL

ABBEY HILL

GROUNDS

To Quarry

Le Brodegate

Alta Strada

'Barn'

Tantara

THE
CASTLE
LOWER POOL

THE
BRAYS

CASTLE

APPROXIMATE SCALE

0   50   100   150   200 Metres

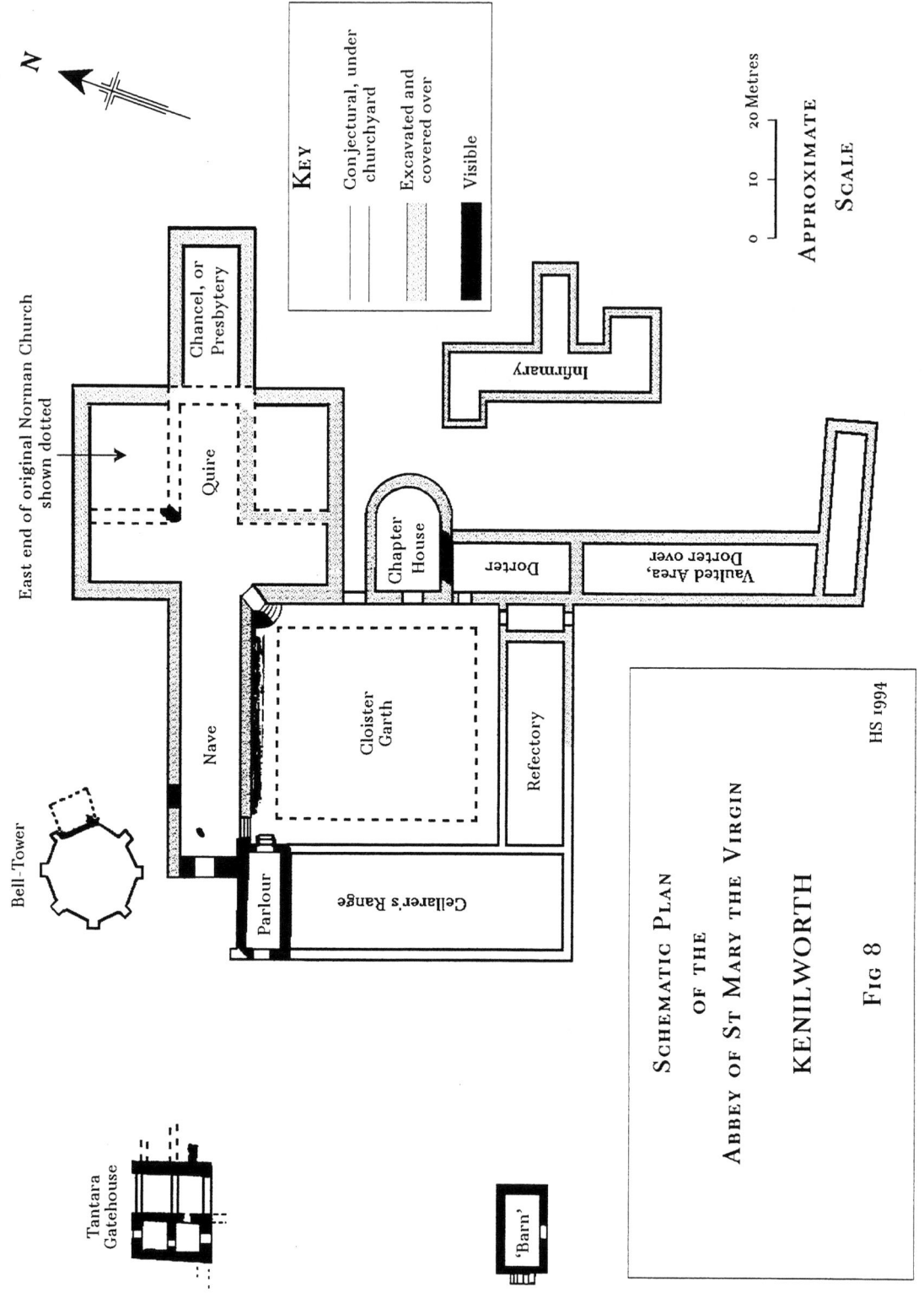

N

KEY

— Conjectural, under
  churchyard

— Excavated and
  covered over

■ Visible

0   10   20 Metres

APPROXIMATE
SCALE

East end of original Norman Church
shown dotted

Chancel, or
Presbytery

Quire

Bell-Tower

Nave

Cloister
Garth

Chapter
House

Infirmary

Dorter

Vaulted Area,
Dorter over

Parlour

Cellarer's Range

Refectory

Tantara
Gatehouse

'Barn'

SCHEMATIC PLAN
OF THE
ABBEY OF ST MARY THE VIRGIN

KENILWORTH

FIG 8

HS 1994

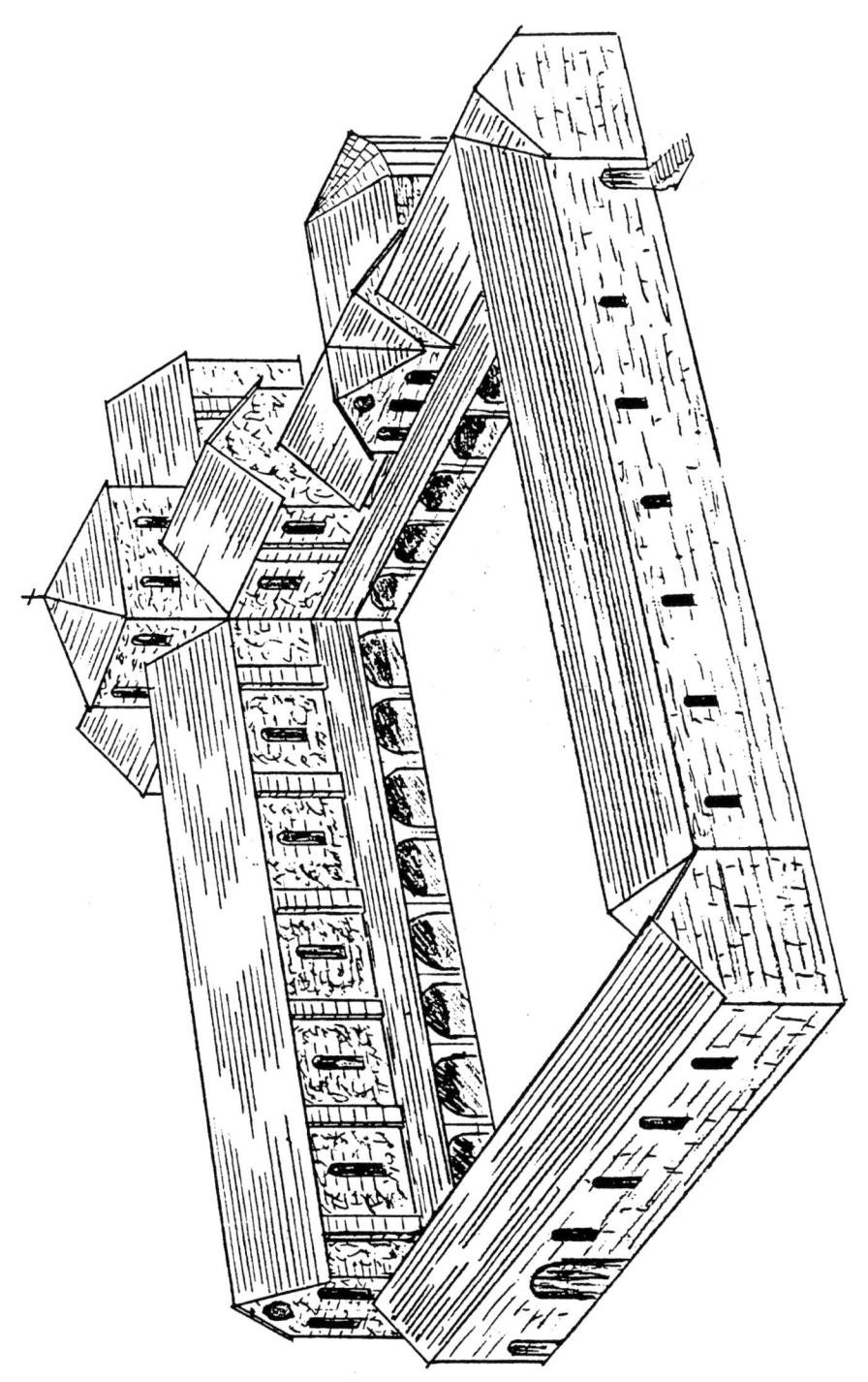

Conjectural Layout of Early Priory

derived from excavation ground plan

This reconstruction must be, necessarily, controversial as there are few extant examples to follow. The above shows the Priory as it may have appeared before the extensive 13th century changes, when the Bell Tower was built, the Transepts trebled in length and a new Chancel added, the Dorter extended, and the Gatehouse and 'Barn' were built

Fig 9

FIG 10A

FIRST KNOWN SEAL OF THE PRIORY, *c* 1235 ~ 9

The full inscription was

SIGILLUM:ECCLESIE:SCE:MARIE:DE:CHINELEWRDA

(Based on *Kenilworth Illustrated*, it has been touched up
to show the west end of the church)

FIG 10B

SEAL OF 1538

Based on *Kenilworth Illustrated*

SAMUEL AND NATHANIEL BUCK'S ENGRAVING OF THE RUINS OF KENILWORTH ABBEY, 1701

Despite being entitled *The East View of Kenilworth Priory*, it is a view from the north. The 'Tantara' Gatehouse is on the right, with the 'Barn' behind it. The remains in the centre of the picture are part of the Cellarer's range, and on the far left is a part of the Chapter House south wall, which still stands today, but without the sculpted decoration shown here. In the left foreground are the remains of the east end of the Church.

FIG 11

To the Right Honourable the Earl of Clarendon

this View of the PRIORY GATE, KENILWORTH, is Inscribed

by his Lordships most Humble Servant William Byrne

Engraved by W. Byrne

London, Published as the Act directs, Dec. 1, 1816, by W. Byrne, N. 79 Titchfield Street.

FIG 12

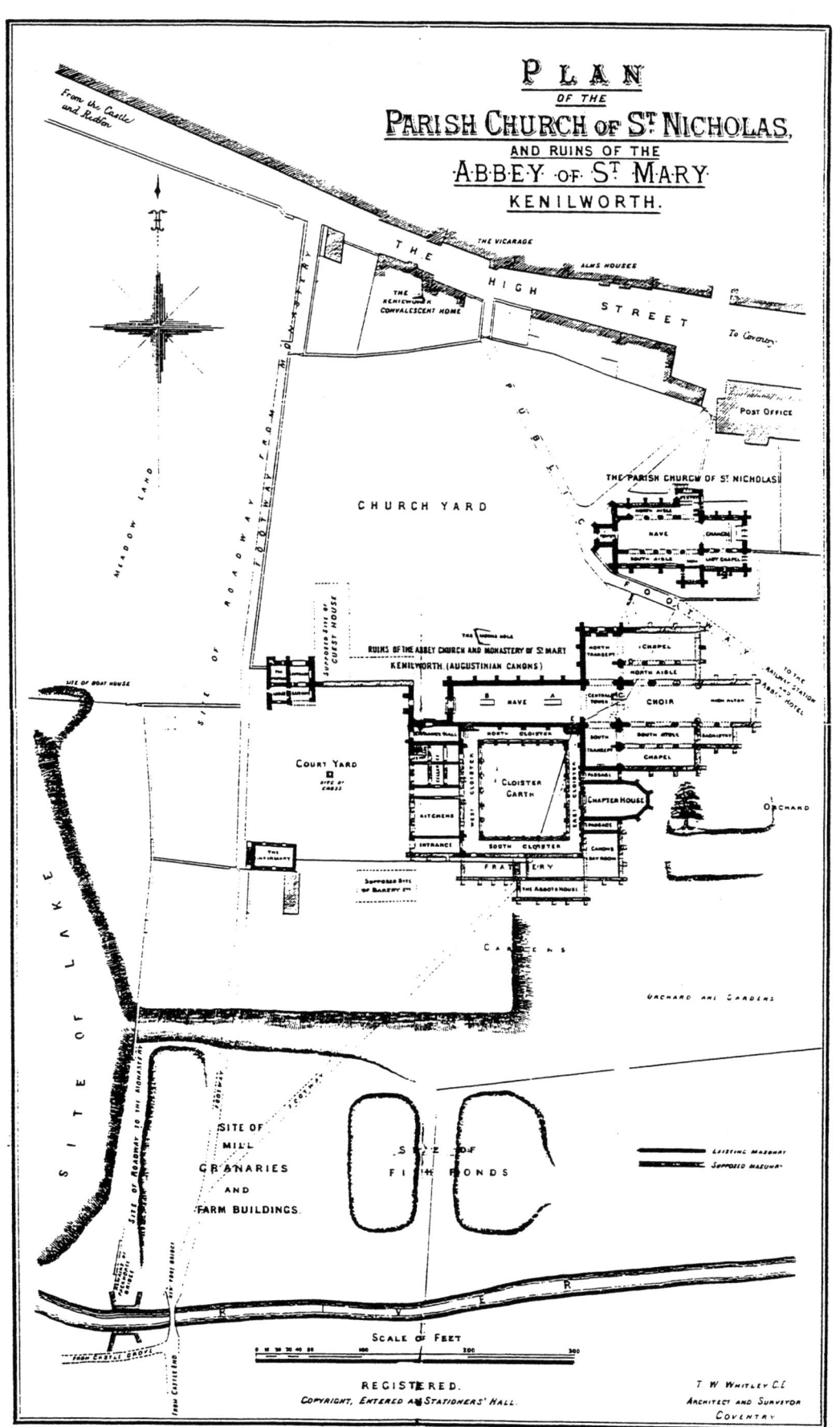

Fig 13

The 'Barn' from the South-East, c 1925

The original use of this 14th century building is uncertain. The entrance to the first floor was at the side, up a stairway now removed, but the scar of where it was is still to be seen. The timber-slots for a porch can be seen around the door at the front. The gable-ends and roofing are post-Dissolution. The building now houses the extant loose remains of the Abbey.

Fig 14A

The 'Barn' at the latter end of the nineteenth century

Fig 14B

St Nicholas' Church Doorway

This array of Norman sculptures from the Priory was assembled at the west end of the Church sometime between 1550 and 1620, to form a façade in the architectural style of the Renaissance period. As such, it is unique

Photograph by courtesy of Nick Dalton

Fig 15

A view northwards along the eastern Cloister range. In the foreground are the
foundations of the later Dorter, then the old Dorter, and the Chapter House south
wall rising beyond. St Nicholas' Church is in the background

FIG 16A

A view westwards over the excavated Chapter House, showing the coffins supposed to
be those of the de Clintons The 'Barn' is in the background

FIG 16B

KENILWORTH ABBEY EXCAVATED, *c* 1925

MEDIÆVAL STONE HEADS FROM THE PRIORY

These heads were discovered during excavations, and were housed in the 'Barn', from which they were
stolen in December, 1992. At the time of publication they are still missing.

Leamington Spa police (44 01926 451111) would be pleased to hear of their whereabouts - associated Crime number is SL/10826/92

FIG 17

X THE CELLS OF KENILWORTH

*Your Superior must not think himself fortunate
in having power to Lord it over you.*

The Rule of St Augustine, VII.3

Few Augustinian Houses had daughter houses or cells subordinate to them. Nostell (Yorks) had four, Kenilworth three, and a few others had one. Most cells became independent, as indeed did Kenilworth's cells at Stone and Calwich; only Brooke remained dependent – until, it seems, 1536.

Dependent houses were not a formal part of the Augustinian system, and may only have arisen through convenience. For instance, the church of Stone in Staffordshire was granted to the canons; then, for whatever reason, the canons manned it themselves, rather than appoint a priest to do so. In such circumstances, more than one canon would have had to be sent, necessitating a clergy-house which formed the nucleus of a cell. This may well have been the general way cells developed, one criterion being distance from the convent; cells also normally had a prior, but as will be seen below, other titles were used. Whilst under the jurisdiction of the mother house, the cells were wholly dependent on it, and manned from it.

STONE

The Cell lies in what is now Lichfield Street in Stone. In the cellar of a house named 'The Priory', there is a rib-vaulted undercroft, a part of the west cloister range, with possible remains of the Chapter House to the east.

The church at Stone was included in a grant to the canons by Geoffrey de Clinton. The canons of Stone soon resented the authority of Kenilworth and sought independence. Thus in 1290, the Bishop of Coventry and Lichfield ordained that Stone became independent of Kenilworth, which retained the patronage, however. Thus the Prior of Kenilworth was required to visit Stone once a year with 10 horses and carriages for a two-day stay, but without bringing or taking away any canons. Whenever the priorship of Stone fell vacant, the Prior of Kenilworth, as patron, gave licence for the election of a successor, holding custody of the cell (and presumably its temporalities) whilst it remained vacant. The election of the new prior was to be overseen by two Kenilworth canons. In return, when the Kenilworth priorship became vacant, the Prior of Stone attended the Chapter House for the election of the new prior. Also, Kenilworth released all rights to the churches held by Stone, in return for a pension of £9 as patrons.

This state of affairs appears to have lasted only until the following year when again differences needed settling. New agreement was reached whereby Kenilworth dropped all claims except that of patronage, for which it received a pension of 12½

marks sterling (approximately £9, as before). Stone acquired the usual privileges; the VCH for Staffordshire comments that it had the right to hang thieves on private gallows.

Stone figured again in Kenilworth's destiny. In 1426, there was a disruption at Kenilworth when the sub-prior was in opposition to the Prior, Thomas Kidderminster, to whom he had been obstinate and 'contumacious'. The sub-prior was sent to Brooke, and two of his cronies, Brothers Thomas Holygreve and Roger Stone, were sent to Stone in disgrace. In fact, there is some doubt about this story; a Kenilworth Library copy of the VCH[41] has been amended in manuscript to the effect that it was Thomas Holygreve who sent the sub-prior to Brooke, in 1446, and only Roger Stone was sent to Stone. This one copy of the VCH is a photo-copy of a somewhat tattered volume in which these comments were originally written. This alternative account is, in part, supported by the Staffordshire VCH which gives Thomas Holygreve as elected Prior of Stone in 1423, three years before he was alleged to have been sent there in disgrace. Thomas Holygreve had a distinguished career in the order, *see* under '1439' in 'Who's Who'.

Stone had its own problems when, in the 1440s, the common life broke down, and the canons did much as they pleased. The causes were the canons' dissatisfaction over allowances and their plots in the conventual garden. The dispute was taken to the Archbishop's Court, and the Prior, Thomas Wyse, was required to institute certain new rules. He refused to do so, however, and was excommunicated. The sentence was lifted when he appealed to Rome on the grounds that the rules were contrary to those statutes and customs to which he had sworn. Nevertheless, the Bishop of Coventry and Lichfield and Prior Thomas Holygreve of Kenilworth descended on Stone to exact from the Prior a promise to institute the rules, which presumably he did. Some of these are of interest, as they indicate some of the problems, and the customs:

> *Each canon to receive an allowance of £1 13s 4d a year for clothes and necessities* (this allowance being the same as for Kenilworth, Darley and Lilleshall Priories. The Augustinian Rule, incidentally, states: 'amongst you, there can be no question of personal property.')
> *The garden plots to be allocated annually, and the profits now applied communally.*
> *The officers of the Priory to be appointed on the advice of the community.*
> *The Priory seal to be kept under the locks of the Prior, Sub-prior and Sacrist.*

Reverence to be shown to the Prior at all times.
Silence to be observed in the choir, cloister and
dormitory.   On Mondays, Wednesdays and
Thursdays, a recreation hour to be allowed before
Vespers when the canons may stroll, read or play
suitable games.
Canons missing matins to be punished by fines
and penitential diet.
The chief days of abstinence to be Friday and
Saturday, and less food to be taken on Mondays
and Wednesdays unless feast days.   Eating and
drinking in the cells to be forbidden.
No canon to leave the precinct without the Prior's
special permission.

At the Dissolution, Stone had a value of £119 14s
11d, and, at its height (1381), had 10 canons.
Kenilworth continued to nominate and present the
Prior of Stone, for which it received, at the time of the
Dissolution, £9 11s 4d a year.

BROOKE

The small house of Brooke was situated on the north-
facing slope of a stream, the Gwash. There are no
visible remains of the Priory in this remote area.
Brooke was the only religious house to have been
founded in Rutlandshire, which is now, temporarily, it
is hoped, a part of Leicestershire.

The first mention of the Priory of St Mary's, Brooke
in Rutland, is *c* 1160 when Henry II confirmed that
the manor of Brooke had been granted to the canons,
the Prior being the Lord of the Manor. It was a small
house, comprising a prior and two canons, its poverty
causing frequent resignations of the prior. In 1298,
Bishop Oliver Sutton of Lincoln (in whose diocese it
was) begged the Prior of Kenilworth to do something
about the state of the house. He complained that the
prior was frequently absent, the house was dilapidated
and decayed and was a scandal to the neighbourhood,
the revenues were mismanaged and the canons and
their servants would soon be begging in the street.
The Prior of Kenilworth, Robert Salle, brushed this
off as exaggeration.   In the 1426 problems at
Kenilworth (*see* Stone, above), the contumacious sub-
prior, Thomas Norton, was sent to Brooke.   As
mentioned in Chapter VI, the nearby church of St
Peter's (about 1.5 Km away and appropriated to
Kenilworth) was required to be served by either a
canon of Kenilworth or of Brooke.

Unusually, Brooke remained a cell of Kenilworth
until just before the Dissolution. In 1536, Thomas
Cromwell, the Vicar General, appears to have leant
on William Wall, the Abbot, to let an unspecified
friend of his have the lease of the manor of Brooke.
Moreover, the Abbot gave a bond of 1000 marks for
the friend's surety. In March 1536, Abbot Walle
wrote to Cromwell complaining that his friends were
encouraging the canon there to rebel against
allegiance to Kenilworth.   This canon, Roger
Harwell, the last prior, surrendered the title of Brooke

manor to the King, because he was dissatisfied with
his allowance. Abbot Walle wrote again to Cromwell
on 18 June, asking him to use his influence to return
Brooke to Kenilworth – or at least be paid a
reasonable rent for it, as the Abbey was getting into
financial difficulty.   When a commission visited
Brooke in June 1536, they found only one canon,
described as a prior. The rest, they were told, had
been recalled by Abbot Walle to Kenilworth. As
Brooke was not listed among the assets of the late
Monastery of Kenilworth by the Augmentation Office
in 1539, it must be assumed that the Abbot never
recovered it.

CALWICH

Nicholas, the son of Nigel and Margerie, before 1126,
granted the Kenilworth canons the hermitage at
Calwich, on the north slope of the river Dove, by the
Derby boundary of Staffordshire. It developed into a
cell of Kenilworth, limited to three canons. The Prior
of Kenilworth had complete control in appointing and
removing the cell's canons, and also presenting the
canon-in-charge to the bishop, on the nomination of
Lord Longford. The position of canon-in-charge was
upgraded to prior by 1259, as "Nicholas, the Prior"
(of Calwich), was appointed Prior of Kenilworth.

Calwich sought independence, and in 1293 challenged
the right of Kenilworth to remove its prior. In 1334
there was further dispute when the Prior of
Kenilworth recalled its superior, now termed its
'Keeper'. The bishop upheld Kenilworth's right, but
it would seem that the Keeper, William Boyden,
'went missing' because in 1336 a warrant was put out
for his arrest. When found, he was to be returned to
Kenilworth, to be *chastised according to the*
discipline of his order. By 1349, Calwich became
independent – at the cost of an annual pension of £3
paid to Kenilworth; this continued until the
Dissolution. The patronage of the nearby church of
Ellastone was transferred from Kenilworth to
Calwich on independence. In 1384, there were a prior
and two canons, all aged and feeble, and the priory
was very poor. Nevertheless, Thomas Dawkins, the
Prior, became prior of the Warwickshire Augustinian
house of Arbury in 1507. There was only one canon
at the Dissolution.

HUGHENDEN

Mention must be made of Hughenden, (or
Hitchenden). According to the guide of *St Michael*
and All Angels, Hughenden, the manor was given by
Henry I to Geoffrey de Clinton, Geoffrey building the
first church between 1100 and 1135. It then adds that
Geoffrey or his successor made over the manor to the
Priory of Kenilworth as an endowment, *"and it seems*
that the monks (sic) *established a small priory"*.
Geoffrey granted the manor to the canons in 1126/7,
but no support has yet been found for the suggestion
that they founded a priory or a cell there.

XI THE RAISING TO ABBEY STATUS

There was not in the world a more pure,
more honest, and more holy creature,

Polydore Vergil on Henry VI

The raising of an Augustinian house from a priory to an abbey was an unusual distinction; in England, unlike the Continent where the order was more structured, there were few Augustinian abbeys, and hence the raising of a priory to abbey status was all the more rare. Of more than 200 Augustinian houses, 32 were founded as, or became abbeys, but one demoted itself, and one changed order. Of the 32, 13 were Victorine and Arrouasian, of continental origin and always founded as abbeys. Of the remaining 19 independent Augustinian houses, 9 were founded as abbeys, for a variety of reasons, including two that had royal patronage, and the rest raised from priories to abbeys; of these, most were raised in the 12th century, soon after foundation, but four were raised later.

Unlike Norton, there is no contemporary charter or other documentary evidence extant for when Kenilworth's upgrading took place. The oft-quoted date is 1458, as this is the first time an Abbot, John Yardley, was elected. Carey-Hill[5] gives an earlier date on the basis of a reference to Abbot Thomas Holygreve in a charter of 1454 concerning the rectory at Bidford. A closer analysis of charters and letters show that up to 1446, the superior was referred to as the prior. There is a draft papal letter of between March 1447 and 1448 (the draft bore no calendar date) which refers to the Pope having been petitioned by the Prior of Kenilworth. The first mention of an abbot so far found is an instruction of 11th July, 1450 from the Pope, addressed to the Bishop of Coventry, and the Abbots of Stoneleigh and Kenilworth, regarding St Michael's church, Coventry. This is followed by the 1454 reference mentioned above. The upraising is thus narrowed down to between 1447 and 1450.

Recently, one of the authors[34] derived a date of 1447. This is based on an entry in *Kenilworth Illustrated*[26] stating that Thomas Savage was appointed Prior in 1447. Thomas Holygreve was elected Prior in 1439 and continued as Superior until 1458; thus Thomas Savage can only have been a prior if the Superior had by now become an Abbot. However, the only reference to Thomas Savage, found so far, is in the *Catalogus Priorum* given in *Kenilworth Illustrated*, where no source is given. Until this source is found – assuming it exists – this evidence must be regarded as a little suspect; it is compatible, however, with the 1447 – 1450 bracket above.

As evidence for Kenilworth's upraising, Greene[18] cites a draft letter of Pope Nicholas V (mentioned above) in the Calendar of Papal Letters of 1447-8 in response to a petition from the Prior and Convent of Kenilworth. This petition requests the renewal of the letters granted by Honorius II to the late Prior Bernard, concerning the right to use the ring and almuce, but not seeking the mitre. However, as Prior Bernard and Honorius II are both 12th century figures, the matter is irrelevant, except that papal interest in the Priory at this time might be significant.

Greene has studied why the Augustinian Priory of Norton (Runcorn) was raised to Abbey status. One group of priories was raised in the 12th century, on the grounds of size and/or royal patronage. Thereafter the pattern became sporadic – Creake 1231, Norton 1391, Kenilworth c 1447 and Bruton 1511. Greene suggests four possible factors in the case of Norton – size of the community, its wealth, the social rôle of the prior and the status of the patron; another factor was the advantage to an impoverished papacy of the sale of this privilege.

The size and wealth of the Kenilworth community were well in the upper band, and it thus would have the necessary qualification – as would indeed many other houses. The authors have held the view that the patronage of Kenilworth was almost certainly the prime consideration, influenced possibly by the standing of the then Prior, Thomas Holygreve. The patronage, as shown in Chapter III, was of course, royal.

Henry VI came to the throne in 1421 aged 9 months, and was crowned king in 1429. One of his favourite resorts was the Abbey of Bury St Edmunds, where he was admitted to the fraternity. He was also fond of Coventry where he often stayed, as well at Kenilworth, where he kept Christmas in 1437. In 1450 he fled to Kenilworth at Cade's Rebellion with his Queen, Margaret of Anjou. He was a deeply religious man and dubbed as 'neither a fool, nor very wise'.

According to the *Dictionary of National Biography*, Henry VI made a tour of monasteries during the summer of 1446. Efforts to find his whereabouts in that year have shown, so far, that he was at Westminster much of the year, but that there is a lack of documents issued by the King from there during August and much of September. Evidence of where he visited is so far lacking, but during this time he may have discovered that he was not only patron, but also dubbed founder of Kenilworth, and considered such distinction befitted abbey status. Of other Augustinian houses of royal (Henry I's) foundation, Carlisle had been raised to cathedral status by 1133, and Cirencester and Wellow-by-Grimsby were founded as abbeys; only Dunstable remained a priory – but an important one. Another precedent was to be found at the Augustinian Priory of Creake in Norfolk.

It was founded in 1227 by Sir Robert de Nerford who died shortly afterwards. His widow, concerned that the benefits bestowed by Sir Robert and herself might be pillaged by their descendants, granted her right of patronage to the Crown. Henry III, in return, confirmed its possessions, and raised it to abbatial rank.

Coupled with the foundation aspects, the Prior, Thomas Holygreve, may have played no small part in the honour bestowed. He seems to stand a head above the other Kenilworth priors (*see* Who's Who, 1439), and had become widely known.

Thus pending further evidence, it is concluded that Kenilworth was raised to abbey status *c* 1447, on account of its royal patronage and 'foundation', coupled possibly with the eminence of its Prior.

There is no evidence of the direct effect that this raising had on the house. The Abbot was not mitred, nor was he summoned to Parliament. There may have been a building programme to meet the prestige requirements of this higher status – Abbot's quarters, for instance. More would also have been required of the Abbot himself, by his Royal Patron in particular. Unfortunately, insufficient accounts are available to determine whether there was a sudden improvement in the house's finances, but Greene investigated this for Norton, and found no evidence. The general indication is that Kenilworth became poorer, possibly due directly to a financial burden associated with the higher status, and also through mismanagement.

XII THE DISSOLUTION

Whether ... the monastery or the practice
of religion is declining

Matters to be investigated by a visiting prelate.
Constitutions of Pope Benedict

The Dissolution of the monasteries was no sudden affair; it had been preceded by many decades of unrest, both within the religious houses and without. By the end of the 13th century, by which time most monastic houses had been founded, there was an acceptable economic balance between the supported monasteries and the supporters. Two waves of the Black Death, in 1349 and 1361, had a profound effect on both monastic life and life outside, and by 1371 the General Order of the Augustinians was expressing concern about apostates – canons who had renounced their order and even their faith. It was decreed that any canon of the order might arrest and imprison them. Salter[31] suggested that the spirit of restlessness aroused by the Peasants' Revolt of 1381 was at work in the monasteries. The general morale of the Church was not bolstered by the Great Schism of the late 14th Century when there were two popes, causing John Wycliffe, to attack the constitution of the church, and later, church dogma. The following incidents indicate some general deterioration from the high ideals of the earlier canons:

1361: under Prior John de Peyto, the state of Kenilworth Priory had apparently become notorious and the King directed the Bishop to investigate. John had been Prior since 1345 and had ruled the house during the 1349 plague and its aftermath, and may by now have been quite old. The nature of the notoriety is not known.

1364: when the Prior of Evesham came to visit Studley Priory (Warwickshire) in lieu of a bishop (the see being vacant), he was threatened with blows; he was only allowed to enter on threatening to excommunicate the canons. This was a part of a general hostility towards Visitations that had been reported to the Chapter of the Order.

1380: the Chapter of the Order again became concerned about apostasy, and in 1383 raised a levy of ½d in the pound for expenses incurred in the Roman Court in connection with such dangers to the order that it was *not expedient to describe*. Salter suggests that this was in connection with bishops, in effect, luring away promising young canons for other office, exempting them from their vow of obedience.

1389: at Kenilworth, John de Coventre became apostate, also stealing from the Prior and another inmate.

1399: at Maxstoke Priory (Warwickshire), one canon killed another in claimed self-defence.

1426: There was further recorded unrest at Kenilworth when the bishop removed the sub-prior for being contumacious, and sent him and two other canons to other houses, as detailed in Chapter X.

1431: the Chapter of the Order was yet again concerned about apostates, and regulations were drawn up for their arrest. Recommendations were made for building monastery prisons. Rebellious canons were to be directed to other houses. By the early 16th century, attendance at the General Chapter itself had become lax.

1439: the Augustinian Priory of Christ Church, London, had suffered misrule, and the common life had broken down at Stone, now independent of Kenilworth.

1518: Cardinal Wolsey wrote to the Chapter stating that the Augustinian Order was in danger and threatened with speedy ruin, and, to help, proposed to build a college for students of the order (a College of St Mary, Oxford).

At Kenilworth, the reports of visitations in 1518, 1521 and 1524 by the Bishop's representative indicate some unrest. Each canon was interviewed in the Chapter House, and, whilst there was a general concensus in support of the Abbot, there was complaint that he had too many servants. There was also criticism of the severity of the Prior and Sub-prior (the superiors), who had charge of the day-to-day running of the Abbey. The canons felt they were given insufficient freedom, and that the punishments were too harsh. An accusation was made that superiors allowed women into their cubicles. A cause of much concern was canon John Rogers (*see* Who's Who), inasmuch as he, while critical of a drop in standards, at the same time complained of the severity of the punishments handed out.

There was thus a general trend of deterioration from the high ideals of the 12th and 13th Centuries. Baugh[2], in referring primarily to the Augustinian house of Haughmond in Shropshire, states that *regular religious discipline had been long and insidiously corroded ..... by the departmentalisation of finances* (that is, the individual officers being assigned specific rents from the abbey's lands), *by paying the canons clothing allowances and salaries, and by domestic and financial separation of the abbot or prior from his fellow canons.* In the case of another Augustinian house in Shropshire, Wombridge, the prior combined his office with that of warden of a collegiate church, and vicar of another church.

Coupled with these internal strains, the church was being subjected to inroads into its very practices; in the last quarter of the 14th century, John Wycliffe attacked the church for deviating from its biblical roots and called for a reformation. Whereas Wycliffe, rector of Lutterworth, died within his parish of a stroke, his followers, the Lollards, were not as fortunate, hundreds being burnt at the stake for heresy, many at Coventry. In 1506, the Prior of the Augustinian House of St Osyth (Essex) had been converted to Lollardism, but was forced to abjure.

Trevelyan [40] sums up the situation nicely when he says ......*the ascetic ideal, which had founded monasteries long ago, was no longer either admired by the world or practised by the monks. Not only did the man in the street have this concern but some of the reforming clergy also, who felt that monastic wealth would be better used for education and religion.* At the same time, Henry VIII's coffers were empty as a result of war with France, and he had little chance of raising funds through taxation. The solution was clear; disband the monasteries and sell the assets.

In 1534, there were over 600 religious houses in the country, housing some 7000 professed monks, canons and friars and 2000 nuns, and their net income was £135,000. The 1534 Act of Supremacy declared Henry VIII and his successors to be the *only supreme head on earth of the Church of England.* The religious houses of Warwickshire, with the exception of the Coventry Carthusians who put up light resistance, acquiesced to the Act. This was in contrast with opposition in the north of the country where, for instance, a number of canons of the Augustinian house of Cartmel in Lancashire were executed for joining the Pilgrimage of Grace, protesting against the Dissolution. Thomas Cromwell was appointed the King's Vicar-General and his commissioners were authorised to visit all cathedrals, churches, colleges, monasteries and other ecclesiastical places with the same power as had previously been held by bishops.

The reports of these unscrupulous commissioners led to the suppression of the lesser monasteries in 1536, 'lesser' meaning an income below £200. The Bill for their dissolution starts with an *apologia*, thus: *For as much as manifest sin, vicious, carnal and abominable living is daily used and committed among the small abbeys, priories, and other religious houses of monks, canons and nuns, ...* Exaggerated, it would nevertheless have had popular appeal. Thus in this first wave of dissolution, the Warwickshire houses of Alcester, Alvecote, Henwood, Pinley, Maxstoke, Stoneleigh Abbey, and probably Arbury, Studley and Warwick (St Sepulchre) Priories surrendered.

Kenilworth Abbey escaped this first wave as its value on the 'Suppression of Minsters' account was £564 1s 1d, which was slightly higher than the average revenue *per capita* for Augustinian Houses, which itself was about 25% less, on average, than for Benedictine Houses. Meanwhile, Abbot William Walle died on the 3rd of January, 1537, and a canon of the Abbey, Simon Jekys, who was a novice in 1524, was elected in his place. This process was very

rapid, the temporalities being restored to him only a fortnight after election. Any suggestion that Simon Jekys was sympathetic to the Dissolution, especially if a good pension was in the offing, and was rushed into the Abbot's seat, is offset by the Abbey making a payment of £100 to the King to avoid or delay dissolution. There was nothing unusual in this; the nunnery at Polesworth and St Anne's, Coventry purchased royal exemption for £50 and £20 respectively, but their continuation was short-lived.

Despite its considerable income, the Abbey was in financial trouble; in 1518 it had a debt of nearly £400 of which the Abbot paid off £300 personally, only to be landed with an assessed levy for a grant to the King of £500. He had been before the King's Court twice in 1521 to explain the high expenditure of his house. Thus, despite the apparent high income of the Abbey, Simon Jekys wrote just before the Dissolution to Thomas Cromwell, the Vicar General of England, pleading poverty; he had had to lease out all the lands except the park at Rudfyn in order to pay their debts. Why was the Abbey in debt? There is neither a profit and loss account nor a balance sheet, but we know the revenues in 1536 were £638 19s 4d. Thus, although their property was at farm, their income was secure, and presumably collected as £6 a year was being paid to the layman Laurence Grey to act as Receiver General. What of their debts? The last known buildings to have been erected are the 14th century Gatehouse and the 'Barn' as it is known today. Were they still paying off any debt incurred? If it were not a capital charge, had the higher worldly expectations of the Abbot and the canons become excessive? The answer must be left with Trevelyan, who merely states that *the monks had not been good managers of their property, for they were terribly in debt.*

Meanwhile, although not a part of their brief, the Visitors descended on the larger houses, urging their surrender under considerable pressure; a retrospective act was not passed through Parliament until 1539 to legalise this action. On the 15th April, 1538, Kenilworth was the first of the houses in Warwickshire to be dissolved, followed in October by the White Friars (1st October) and Grey Friars (5th) of Coventry, Merevale Abbey (13th), Black Friars of Warwick (20th) and Trinitarian Friars of Thelsford (26th). Then in January 1539, Polesworth Abbey (3rd), the Benedictine Priory (15th), Carthusian Priory of St Anne's (16th) and Coombe Abbey (21st). Then finally on the 12th of September, the nunnery at Nuneaton Priory was closed.

In the surrender document the Kenilworth Abbot and canons voluntarily and unanimously, *for just and reasonable cause*, gave the Abbey to Henry VIII together with all its properties in the counties of Warwickshire, Gloucester, Worcester, Northampton shire, Buckinghamshire, Somerset and Oxford.

The religious of the dissolved houses were pensioned; in the case of Kenilworth, the canons received between £5 and £7 a year, the Prior £8 and the Abbot

£100, compared with the Abbot of Stoneleigh who only received a pension of £23. Analysis shows the relationship between the value of the house and pension of its superior is roughly linear, approximating to 17% of the value of the house, to which Kenilworth conforms. Dugdale tells us 'as he has heard' that Simon Jekys was assigned Rudfyn Manor for his residence whilst he lived. In the light of his short period as Abbot – 15 months – he came out of the Dissolution very well.

The King's Commissioners in due course descended on the Abbey, one of their prime targets being the valuable lead on the roofs which they melted down into 'pigs'. One of these lay hidden until 1888 – no doubt somebody had intended to return to collect it, despite its weight of 10¾ hundredweight (550 Kilogrammes). It now lies by the altar-rail at St Nicholas' church. Removing the roofing became the most effective way of ensuring the rapid deterioration of the structure beneath.

Of the moveable assets, only the Kenilworth Cartulary, the 'Harley 3650' [44], seems to have survived. As this document is concerned with the grants of land, etc, to the Abbey, it was important that it should survive; it would be needed to identify the Abbey Estate for its new owner, initially the Crown.

Analysis [35] of the movement of incumbents in the churches of the Knightlow Hundred shows that some of the canons became parish priests, as follows:

Richard Bager	Harbury	1550
Randolph Baxter	King's Newnham	1559
Thomas Parker	Ashow	1542
Richard Palmer	Wolvey	1564
Richard Todde	Claverdon	1543
William Warwick	Alveston	1549

Of these, Richard Bager was a canon in 1515, and Richard Todde a canon (at Maxstoke) in 1518. The rest were more recent, and having to be 24 years old before becoming a canon, they were no more than in their early forties. The older ones presumably retired on their £5–£7 pension and lived happily ever after; even this small amount represented three times the wages of a labourer.

XIII THE AFTERMATH

Although it could have been wished that the excavations might be completed, or at least that it might not have been necessary to cement the old stones into sham walls, yet we must be grateful to those who have so energetically worked to 'dig up' these new old-new honours for Kenilworth.

W H Draper, 1891

By 1547, according to a survey[21], the church and all the buildings had been defaced. Another survey drew attention to the availability of stone for use at the Castle. It was used there and also became distributed around Kenilworth to build the foundations of dwellings. In 1553, 42 hundred-weights of lead from the Abbey were given by Queen Mary to nearby Rowington church, and in 1557, Rowington paid for the purchase and cartage of stone from the Abbey; this is to be clearly seen today, topping the north aisle of that church. In the 1920s some of the stone was sold to fund an excavation, and is to be found in gardens and rockeries in Kenilworth.

In 1547, the Court of Augmentation, set up specifically for dealing with dissolved religious sites, appointed Bailiffs to account for their associated properties. A detailed document[3] was compiled of properties and tenants, which includes a description of the Abbey site, covered in Chapter IX, which was now let to Andrew Flammock, a knight and courtier who owned other property in the area. He was succeeded by his son, Sir William, who died in 1560, and the site passed to his daughter Katherin aged 2–3 years old. In due course she married John Colbourne of Moreton Morrell. Dugdale[14] imparts a bit of hearsay to the effect that this John bought some horses, after which he was told that they had been stolen from the stables of Robert Dudley, Earl of Leicester, at the Castle. This terrified poor John and as a result he sold the Abbey site to him 'on easy terms'. Thereafter, until 1884, the site descended with the Castle.

Some time between 1550 and 1620[36], probably nearer the latter, pieces of Norman decorative stonework from the Abbey were built into a Renaissance composition to form a west door of St Nicholas' church. Although the format is not Norman, the material is, and it is a fine reminder of the type of decoration the Abbey boasted, (*see*Fig 15).

Samuel Buck, assisted by his brother, Nathaniel, engraved some 340 views of castles and abbeys in his lifetime. Included were representations of the Castle and Abbey circa 1701, the Abbey site being shown to be extensively ruined, although a part of the west cloister wall which is no longer visible was then still standing.

In time, the Abbey ruins, by now little more than foundations, became more or less invisible, the few remains above ground being covered heavily with ivy. The Gatehouse (Fig 12) was still standing, bereft of its roof and upper part, but it was in use as a dwelling;

the fireplace had been modified, and a 1787 print shows smoke from a chimney. Another print of 1787 shows a chimney and a thatched roof. To make the building waterproof, the top was sealed with clay and then thatched. The clay provided the footing for subsequent heavy vegetation. The 'Barn' (Fig 14) lost its roof at the Dissolution, probably for the lead. 50-100 years later, it was re-roofed with re-used timbers. The gables were filled in with brick at the west end, and brick and timber at the east, and it was used as a barn. A fine photograph of the Abbey Fields, of probably 1865 shows the east end of the south face extending southwards, the west side being open; it was probably used as a cowshed. There is mention of this, or an earlier building, in Chapter IX. Another photograph of *c* 1890 also shows a hip-roofed barn alongside it, but both seem to have disappeared soon afterwards. A slightly later photograph shows no evidence of the latter, and by the time of Carey-Hill's report, the only evidence left of them were the beam-slots in the south face of the 'Barn'.

Meanwhile, St Nicholas' Churchyard was encroaching on the Abbey site. Starting on the north side of the church, it had spread westward, on the north side of the footpath that faces the west door. It then spread southwards to turn the corner, and then eastwards, back towards the church. It was here, first in 1793, then in 1840, that ruins were struck under the soil, and so explorations were carried out. Several items were found including sepulchral slabs, floor tiling, window tracery, etc, and also the foundations of a building of octagonal or, at least, semi-octagonal form. Matthew Bloxham, Esq, of Rugby, gave the opinion that the building thus discovered was the Chapter House of the old Abbey. A part of these foundations was left exposed below ground level, a retaining wall being built around; the pit created earned itself the name of 'The Monks' Hole'. Almost certainly a bell-tower, it has been discussed in Chapter IX.

Lightning struck St Nicholas' church spire in 1858, requiring its rebuilding, and in 1865, the church came under restoration. A block of three ogee-headed *sedilia*, which had hitherto been concealed behind wainscotting since the 16th century, were now removed, and were placed, for no obvious reason, so that they jutted out from the west side of the Gatehouse. They were returned to an altered chancel, according to the Reverend John Thomson, in the

1870s, and are happily still there. They are to be seen, however, on some of the earlier photographs of the Gatehouse.

By 1889, the main site of the Abbey was owned by the Parochial Council, and the outer court, including the Gatehouse and the 'Barn', by four local worthies; this part was now bought by the Local Board for £400 for 'public walks and pleasure grounds'. It continued in Council ownership, and is now held by the Warwick District Council, the area of the Abbey church being owned by the Parochial Church Council.

Further problems in extending the churchyard were encountered in the 1880s, and W H St John Hope, Assistant-Secretary of the Society of Antiquaries visited the site, reporting back to a Parish Meeting that, rather than dig over the whole area and remove all the stones, *many of which ..... are a large size,* it would be better to excavate the area properly. As a result, in 1890, and under a Coventry architect, T W Whitley, a committee was formed which undertook an excavation, funded by local subscription. The main achievement of this investigation was a plan – unhappily there was no associated report. Whitley's plan (Fig 13) contained some guess-work which in the light of the later plan was surprisingly accurate. Whitley uncovered the nave of the church and the western end of the transepts and the Chapter House. The solitary length of wall rising some three metres above ground, as it still does today, was an indication of a major feature which proved to be the Chapter House. Having found its apsidal end, Whitley was able to say that the semi-octagonal plinth found in 1840 was indeed the base of a bell tower.

A Mr W H Draper visited the Abbey site during the 1890 excavation, and reported [13] that .... *among the debris were many pieces of old stained glass, some of which I carefully washed in order to copy the colours, and where possible the pattern: these however, are far too few and small to be of any permanent interest.* During the 1922 excavation, a schoolboy, Joseph Clifford, was given the job, with his peers, of picking up glass that was scattered around an area east of the Chapter House and south of the South Transept. In 1972, whilst cleaning out the 'Barn', a pile of broken glass was found in a corner. Fortunately it was examined before disposal, and found to be mediæval stained and painted glass. A total of 1061 pieces were recovered, many of which are very eroded and fragile, but 521 have been drawn in detail and reported [39].

The final excavation was started in 1922 under another architect, Joseph Crouch, using the balance of the Prince of Wales' local fund for the relief of the poor. The result of that excavation was reported by E Carey-Hill [5], a local man of some eminence (*see* the Appendix for a short biography). Unfortunately, much of the material found is unrecorded; Chatwin [7] mentions that floor tiles were removed before the pattern was recorded, ...*unfortunately necessitated by the thieving propensities of some visitors who came to see the progress of the excavation in 1922.*

This excavation uncovered the east end of the church, the east wing of the cloister with its extension, and the part of the south wing not in the churchyard. The Fermery and part of another building were also uncovered. Alfred H Gardner, FRIBA, a Kenilworth resident then in his early twenties, was articled to Joseph Crouch, and was commissioned to prepare the plan of the layout. This plan was the major achievement of that excavation and was used as the basis of Figure 8. Not all the site has been exposed, mainly because the churchyard now lies over most of the south and west sides of the cloister and any attendant buildings. In the very dry summer of 1976, the outline of further buildings, seen where the grass had died, were recorded [9].

Some, and indeed it may be much, of the material excavated has disappeared. Of that extant, most was put in the 'Barn' and some in St Nicholas' church. This is now all in the 'Barn'. Carey-Hill's report shows items no longer available, and Philip Chatwin [6] identified two coffin lids, now in the Crypt of St Mary's, Warwick, which almost certainly came from the Abbey. There is, incidentally, a fine coffin-lid figure of a canon, essentially complete except for his damaged head, exposed in the north transept area of the Abbey church. This should be removed to a less exposed location.

It is ironic that contemporary with the 1922 excavations, the site of the fish ponds, as shown on Whitley's plan to the south of the main buildings, were being covered over with lawn tennis courts, now hard courts.

St Nicholas' Churchyard, and the parts of the Abbey within it, had been enclosed by walling, most of it with railings, and gates; the only ungated access was the path from opposite the Vicarage, on the north side of High Street, to the west door of the church. The railings were removed under compulsory order in 1942, or thereabouts, to make munitions; only their stumps still grace the wall. The gates have now also gone.

Concern about the condition of the Gatehouse was expressed by His Majesty's Office of Works in 1931, which estimated a cost of £980 for repair, but the following year the Council decided the time was inappropriate to raise the money. Later attempts were delayed by World War II, and it was not until the 1970s that Kenilworth Abbey Advisory Committee, under the chairmanship of Alfred Gardner, mentioned above, raised £20,000, and the building was consolidated. The committee was an independent voluntary body, comprising representatives from the Kenilworth Society, the Kenilworth History & Archæology Society, and the Town and District Councils.

When the Local Board acquired the bulk of the Abbey Fields between 1884-9, the 'Barn' become a storeroom, but in 1932 'The Friends of Kenilworth Abbey' were formed, and in 1937 an exhibition of Abbey material was mounted there. Carey-Hill prepared a shortened guide to the Abbey, recently reprinted[5]. However, the War intervened, and the 'Barn' again became a council storeroom, along with Abbey artefacts. Early in the 1970s, the Council invited the Kenilworth History & Archaeology Society to catalogue the contents, which led to a major clear-up, and shortly afterwards it manned a free exhibition on Sunday afternoons in the summer – and still does. The Abbey Advisory Committee was re-formed in 1988 to promote the Abbey as a tourist attraction and, in particular, to raise money for the re-instatement of the first floor in the 'Barn' to allow a better exhibition of the finds.

During the 1922 excavation, two lidless coffins, one complete and one broken, were unearthed from the Chapter House; they were assumed to be those of the founder, Geoffrey de Clinton and his son, but this is far from certain (*see* Chapter XIV). In October, 1936, a report leaked out, to the acute embarrassment of the Council, that the coffin that was complete had been smashed up in the 1920s by a workman who had misunderstood his instructions. Both broken coffins are now in the 'Barn'.

The problem of the exposed ruins came to a head in 1964 when brambles and other vegetation were causing damage to the stone-work. The Rev John (Jack) Thomson, Vicar of St Nicholas' and keen Abbey historian, led a group on Sunday afternoons to clear the ruins; this group unhappily dwindled rapidly, and there was no recourse but for the Council to cover them over in 1967 for protection. A series of slides of *c* 1922 exists, but, with hindsight, a more comprehensive survey should have been carried out before the ruins were concealed. A great deal of money would be required to re-excavate, as it will have to be accompanied by consolidation of the stone-work.

Maps of the Abbey Fields show an area just south of the swimming pool as 'Priory Mill, Site of'. In January, 1989, Severn Trent Water Authority laid a pipe through the Abbey Fields, exposing stonework in this area. Work was temporarily halted whilst the Warwick County Museum, aided by the Kenilworth History & Archæology Society, did an emergency, or rescue, dig. Some of the stonework was then removed to allow the pipe to be buried. A report is awaited, but it does not seem that the mill itself was uncovered.

Early morning on 21st March, 1990, vandals broke into the 'Barn' and lit a fire of pamphlets and other documents held in it. By the time the Fire Brigade had arrived, an area of wooden benching on which stone-work was displayed, and under which it was stored, was well ablaze. Concerned for the wooden roofing, the Brigade most properly doused the fire with water. Unhappily, this caused much of the hot stone-work to crack.

In December, 1992, thieves entered the 'Barn' and stole 8 splendid medieval stone carved heads that were the centre-piece of the exhibition. Figure 17 shows a print that has been circulated by the local society to centres of medieval sculpture, in the hope that a recovery will be made.

The Kenilworth Abbey site has not yet become a well-known place to visit, although it has points of interest at least as significant as at much better known sites. It is hoped that in the ensuing years this situation will be rectified.

POSTSCRIPT

It is worth pondering for a moment to think of those people who have passed through the west doorway of the nave; canons, priors, abbots, bishops, princes, kings and queens. The stonework, eaves-dropping on conversations, would have heard Anglo-Saxon, Norman- and Anglo-Norman French, Middle and Tudor English. It may be hard to visualise the people of a monastery, but we now know many of their names, and what some of them did, but still have only the faintest of ideas of the people they were. Their basic tradition lasted over 400 years, and had therefore to them, at least, something worth grasping. Today, there are cults, especially in the United States, that imitate the idea of the common life (although chastity does not seem to be one of their tenets). Those genuinely seeking higher ideals must be encouraged; the Augustinians were a significant force in this search, and even today the same Rule and ideals are being applied by monasteries and convents up and down the country: the quality of their application, at least, has not been lost.

XIV GEOFFREY de CLINTON

He taketh up the simple out of the dust, and lifteth
the poor out of the mire; that he may set him
with the princes, even with the princes of his people.

Psalm 113, vv 6 & 7 (1662 BCP)

Kenilworth today is divided by the valley of Finham Brook into two distinct settlements. To the north is High Street, or High Town, as it was still called last century. To the south of the valley is the main town of Kenilworth. The green sward that separates these two communities runs almost uninterruptedly from Echo Meadow to the west of the Castle, right through to the Common and into the eastern countryside towards Coventry. This unique division of the town is a legacy of Geoffrey de Clinton, and is a direct result of his castle and priory, built along the river valley. After their fall, it remained as pasture – the Abbey Meadow, Herse Close, Rushey Meadow, Calves Close – names on the 1692 map by James Fish. There has been encroachment in more recent times – along School Lane and Forge Road. In 1986, the Department of the Environment ill-advisedly allowed a builder's appeal, despite local outcry, for dwellings adjacent to the brook at School Lane. Although no significant building has started (1994), a mill site has been destroyed, and further desecration of the de Clinton legacy is expected.

Of Geoffrey himself, surprisingly little is known. Dugdale [14] was uncertain of his origins, but quoted Rous who referred to him as a grandson of Will de Tankerville, Chamberlain of Normandy, Dugdale adding *but of the certainty thereof I much doubt*. This was John Rous (not Francis 1579-1643), a Warwickshire antiquarian who was at one time priest at the chapel at Guys Cliffe and who died in 1491. Leland wrote in his *Itinerary of England and Wales (1535-43): There ly 3 of the Tancrevilles the father, the sunne and his sun within the Chapitre house of the Priory of Kenelworthe....* This led to the belief that the two coffins in the Chapter House were Geoffrey and his son, Geoffrey II.

As a result of recent collaboration with a Norman colleague, there are now reasonable grounds for supposing that Geoffrey's father was a William de Semilly, from St-Pierre-de-Semilly on the outskirts of St-Lô. William came to England, possibly with, or in the time of, the Conqueror, and in due course became lord of Glympton in Oxfordshire, taking its name, which evolved into Clinton.

Orderic Vitalis, the Anglo-Norman chronicler (1075 – 1143) saw Geoffrey as one of the low-born whom Henry raised from the dust – although how low, he did not say. He became one of the most powerful barons in the land; it was a habit of Henry I to grant land to lowly 'bright young men' to keep them directly dependent upon himself. Watson [44] suggests that Henry I, as Henry Beauclerc, lord of Cotentin, first met Geoffrey in Normandy, before becoming

king; but they were also close neighbours when the King was at Woodstock, as he often was. Geoffrey's seat at Glympton was only 5.5 Km (3 miles) away. In 1110, Henry issued a charter concerning Abingdon Priory from Woodstock, Geoffrey being the last of the witnesses, which included Roger of Salisbury and the Bishop of London. The first evidence of Geoffrey attesting a document is of 1108.

Despite the implication that the de Clintons were the English part of the Semilly family, Geoffrey's son, Geoffrey, according to Dugdale, held the castle of *Simili*. By the time of King John (Jean Sans Terre), like Kenilworth, it was held by the Crown.

Geoffrey became the King's chamberlain, a distinctly intimate rôle that involved total trust and constant companionship. From this position, he became treasurer, probably following Herbert the Treasurer, who was found guilty of treason. During his time as Court Treasurer, which was probably between 1118 and 1122 or 3, the Court of Exchequer came into existence – to replace the informal and less effective administration of William I. Geoffrey continued to appear at Court, and, between 1110 and 1132, attested to at least a further ninety Royal Acts.

Geoffrey held over 60,000 acres in fourteen counties of England, and was sheriff of Warwickshire from about 1120 to his death. As well as Kenilworth, Geoffrey held Brandon Castle, some 12 kilometres east of Kenilworth, which also employed water for defence (the ruined Castle of Semilly today has two meres at its base, but whether they were there in Geoffrey's time is uncertain). There may also have been an early connection between the de Clintons and Fillongley, which has two castles; one of these compares well with Kenilworth and Brandon

In 1130, Geoffrey was arrested at the King's Palace at Woodstock while the King was in Normandy, and was tried by the King's brother-in-law, David, King of Scotland and Earl of Huntingdon. Geoffrey was alleged to have entered Scotland with an armed force of 59 knights. All the chroniclers note the event, and record that the case was dismissed, giving no explanation.

The last recorded appearance of Geoffrey is at Ditton in 1133, and he must have died before the King did (1135), as after 1133 Henry I addressed a letter to Geoffrey's younger brother William as Sheriff of Warwickshire; thus he was acting as head of the family and guardian of young Geoffrey II – still clearly a minor.

As late as 1534, alms were still being given to the poor for Geoffrey's soul, as Founder (despite the

King also having acquired this rôle), and the anniversaries of his son and grandson were also celebrated. Despite Leland's and others' assertions regarding the two Geoffreys being buried in the Chapter House, a current archæological view is that the coffins are of a later date, and that, had the de Clintons been buried at Kenilworth, it would, in any case, have been in the Church, a more important burial place. Further, Geoffrey II purchased land in Newton, near Clifton upon Dunsmore, either for his father's burial or at the time of his father's burial.

The Clinton family tree is shown on Figure 18. It is based on Dugdale, with the cautious additions of William de Semilly as Geoffrey's father, and Osbert as his unnamed brother. One of Geoffrey I's nephews was Bishop of Coventry and Lichfield, often referred to as the Bishop of Chester, an earlier title. He was a man of martial vigour, and died at Antioch in 1148 on the second Crusade. Geoffrey himself had three sons and a daughter, namely Geoffrey II, his heir, and Lescelina, Robert and William, possibly in that order. Geoffrey II married Agnes, the infant daughter of the Earl of Warwick. Lescelina married Norman de Verdun, the son of Bertram who was a Sheriff of Warwickshire. Robert became a canon of Kenilworth, but not, apparently, before having two sons, Simon and Roger. Of William, little is known, apart from his acquiring Glympton from Geoffrey I, which descended through both his sons, Ralph, and then Jordan, who made an exchange such that it was held by Henry de Clinton, Geoffrey's grandson.

From Geoffrey I's brother, assumed to be Osbert, evolved the famous de Clinton line of Coleshill, Maxstoke and Baddesley Clinton who may (dare it be said?) have been the forebears of a certain President of the United States.

The Clintons disappeared from Kenilworth after Henry acquired Lower Swansbourne (*see* Chapter III), but an Avicia Clintone appears at Ashow in the Hundred Rolls of 1279-80 [22] as holding 15 acres of land from William de Semilly, great-grandson of Henry de Semilly, to whom Geoffrey de Clinton granted the manor of Radford Semele.

FAMILY TREE of the early De CLINTONS

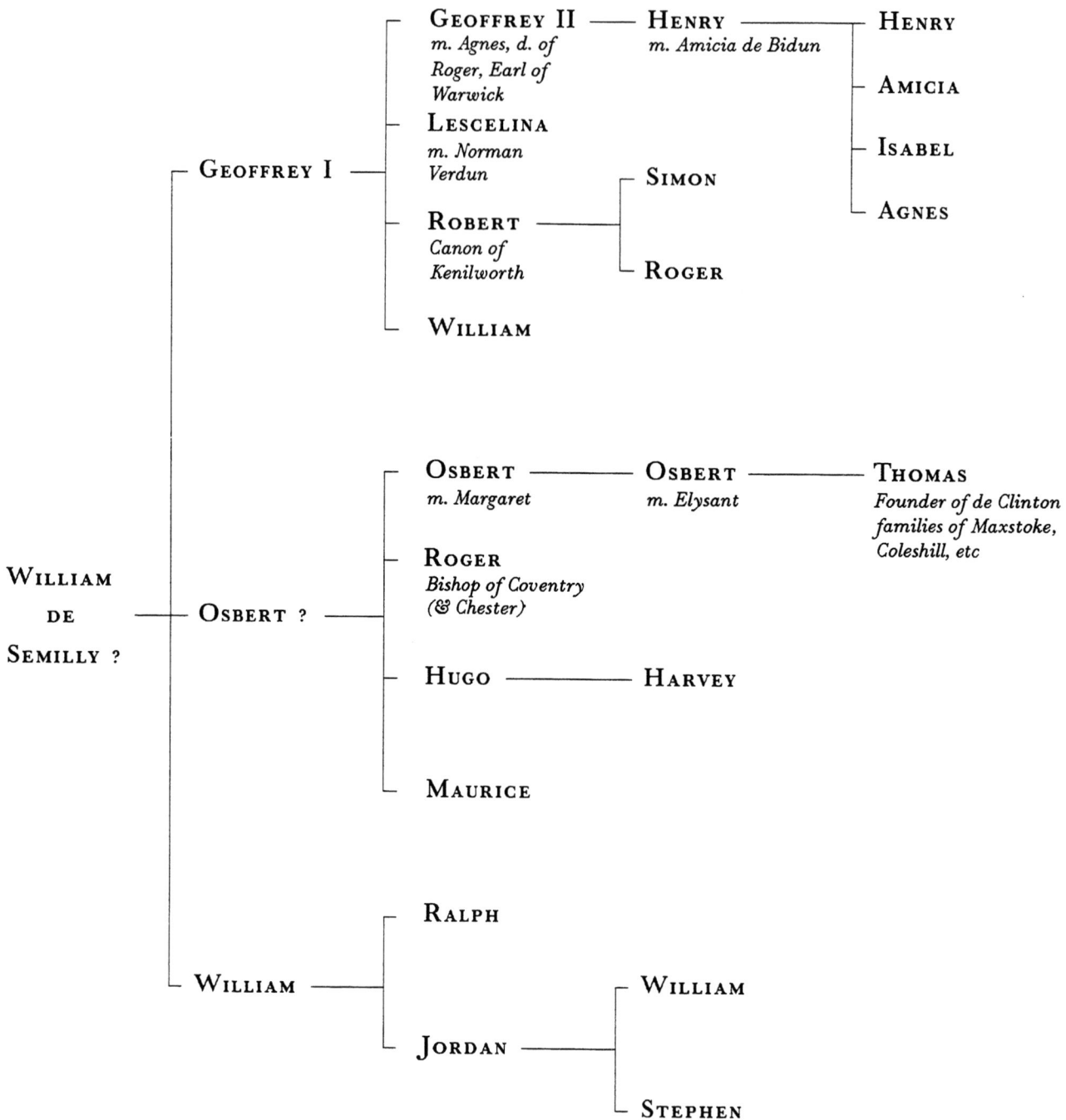

Based on Dugdale, who is very short on dates.
The order in which the offspring are placed is not necessarily correct

FIG 18

APPENDICES

The subjects of these short notes are

complementary to the main text

CONTENTS

1 AUSTIN FRIARS

It is as well to distinguish between the Augustinian Canons and the nominally associated Friars. There is, in fact, little common heritage except for use of 'The Rule'. The origins of the Augustinian or Austin Friars stem from two groups of Italian hermits who, under Pope Innocent IV in 1244, had a Superior General placed over them. In 1256 they were formally instituted as the Order of Friar Hermits of St Augustine, adopting the 'The Rule'. As Friars, they were committed to an itinerant life of preaching and poverty. The first house in England was at Clare, Suffolk, which was founded in 1248. The friaries succumbed to the Dissolution, but there was a revival last century, originating from Ireland, and there are today communities of Austin Friars at Hoxton, in London, in Hythe, Kent and at the original English house at Clare in Suffolk where the priory was reconsecrated in 1954, the original Fermery now being used as the church.

Martin Luther, incidentally, was an Austin Friar.

2 E CAREY-HILL

E Carey-Hill (as he is always known in print) is perhaps best known today for having written the report of the 1922 excavation of the Abbey; there was no report prior to his, and there has been virtually nothing since. His name occurs frequently in association with Abbey and local matters, but little is known today of the man himself. His daughter, Mrs Rosemary Williams, was kind enough to supply information on which the following is based.
Eustace Carey Hill (sic), born in 1882, served in the Boer War and then joined his father at the Coventry firm of Rowland Hill & Sons, aluminium founders. He then spent 25 years at Dartmouth Auto Castings. As well as being an industrialist, he had a life-long interest

in Warwickshire history. He was one-time president of the Coventry Natural History & Scientific Society, a member of the Dugdale Society, and served on the Coventry City Guild of Ancient Buildings and also the Bishop of Coventry's Advisory Committee for the Care of Churches since its inception in 1924. He was a Fellow of the Society of Antiquaries. He wrote many papers on local places of interest, including Kenilworth Castle, on which he was an authority, and Caludon Castle in Stoke, Coventry. A member of several of the Coventry Craft Guilds, he did much work in transcribing their old minutes and other documents. As a Freemason, he was past Master of St Michael's Lodge, Coventry and an Officer of the Grand Lodge of England and the Grand Chapter of England. By 1924, he had researched the 'Brinklow Mound', deducing that it was a motte. At a more local level, he was Honorary Secretary of the Friends of Kenilworth Abbey 1932-34, and later had much to do with the opening of the 'Barn' as an exhibition in 1937. He wrote a visitors' guide to the Abbey (price 6d; reprinted in 1985[5]). He also served on the Kenilworth District Council, terminating his office there in 1931. But it was not all work; in his younger days he was a keen swimmer – quarter-mile champion of Coventry and half-mile champion of Warwickshire. His son, Anthony, a fighter pilot, was killed over the Channel in January 1942. Carey, as he was known to his intimates, lived at the Hollies, New Street, Kenilworth. He died in 1962, the same year, as it happens, that a group in the Kenilworth Society formed what is today the Kenilworth History & Archæology Society.

We have much for which to thank this talented and dedicated man.

3 GEOFFREY de CLINTON'S FOUNDATION CHARTER

The following is based on Latin versions given in Monasticon[15] and the Stoneleigh Leger Book[20].

I, Geoffrey de Clinton, Chamberlain to King Henry give greetings in the Lord to all of the Holy Church of God. Let it be known to all, whether French or English or foreigners or kinsmen, that I, Geoffrey, for the redemption of my sins, and for the salvation of my lord, King Henry, and my wife, sons, relations and friends, have founded the church in Chenilleuurda in honour of St Mary, and I have granted to the canons regular, servants of God, all the open land of the said Chenilleuurda and woodland and all the remaining aforesaid village except those parts I hold for making my castle and enclosed land (or park). Henceforth, I grant them the manors of *Salfort* (Salford Priors), *Itelecota* (Idlicote), and *Niweham* (Kings Newnham) with all their appurtenances, and free and immune from all secular service to the king, myself and my heirs. I have therefore granted them the church of (*Wottona*) Leek Wootton with all that belongs to it, namely one hide in the said Leek Wootton and two hides in *Lilentona* (Lillington) and the church of *Clintona*, (Glympton, in Oxon) and the church of *Bartona* (Barton Seagrave) which is in Northamptonshire, which I have acquired for them. I also grant and steadfastly order that they have their own court and all customary rights and liberties just as I have mine from the King. Concerning pasture, I grant that wherever my cattle or pigs are either within or outside the park, so shall they have their cattle and their demesne pigs. They shall put their tenants' swine from their land in my other woodland outside the park and enclosure, and shall receive pannage from it, just as I receive it from my tenants. All this and anything else I shall acquire in addition for the church, I grant freely and without any obligation of temporal service and secular dues on the part of the servants of God residing in the church, both for the future and the present. I ask, therefore, all the faithful of the Catholic Church, for the love of God and the salvation of their souls to maintain and defend the aforementioned church together with all that is due to it. If, however, my heir (*heres meus*) should attempt to take away or diminish anything that I have granted to the aforesaid church, he shall incur the curse of his father and the anger of God, unless he should retract. If he maintains and supports these canons and their liberties aforesaid which I have granted them, I lease to him and his successors in that they may preserve this, the divine favour and blessing which a father may bestow upon his son and his successors. The witnesses of the grant and decision are; Roger, Bishop of Chester; Roger, Bishop of Salisbury, & Nigel, his nephew; Roger, Earl of Warwick; Ralph Basset; Norman, Prior of London, and Bernard his brother; Gaufridus Luvet; Richard de Torneriis; Aucherus Steward; Nicholas, Clerk; and Nicholas de Rouen, etc.

4 PRIORY AND ABBEY SEALS

The two better known seals are Catalogue [16] Numbers M416 and M417. The first is of *c* 1235-9, and depicts the Virgin, crowned with a nimbus, seated on the roof of the Priory church, holding a sceptre in her left hand, and a book in her right. Figure 10a is a clear representation from *Kenilworth Illustrated*, although more damaged than the less clear version illustrated in the *Victoria County History*. The legend, as given by Dugdale, is:

SIGILLUM ECCLESIE SCE MARIE DE CHINELEWRDA

(Seal of the church of St Mary, Kenilworth).

The question of whether this representation of the church is in fact realistic, and whether the tower on the left side of the church is a bell tower, has been touched on in Chapter IX.

The later Abbey seal, Figure 10b of 1538, just before the Dissolution, is described as: *in a canopied niche of Renaissance design, the Virgin, crowned with nimbus, seated, holding the Child on her left knee and a sceptre in her right hand. On either side of the niche, a waving spray of foliage; below, a shield of arms: quarterly, France modern and England.* The inscription is:

S'COE:MONASTERII:BTE:MARIE: DE:KENNELWORTH

The shield is indicative of the royal patronage of the Abbey.

As for the other known seals, reference 16 includes, Prior Thomas' seal (1339, catalogue number M419) and Prior Robert's seal (1423, M420). Thomas de Warmington's seal depicts the Annunciation, and Prior Robert's seal depicts the Prior kneeling before St Helen. However, the Prior in 1423 was Thomas Kidderminster, so either the given name is wrong, or it was Robert de Salle's seal (1292-1312) being used at a later date. This is, of course, very unlikely, as Thomas Kidderminster's seal would have superseded Robert de Salle's and made it obsolete.

5 SAINT AUGUSTINE OF HIPPO AND HIS RULE

Aurelius Augustinus was born in 331 in the small Roman town of Tagaste, in Numidia, North Africa. Son of a Christian mother, Monica (later canonised), and a pagan father, Patricius, Augustine had no formal baptism as a child. Following a good grounding in grammar, he went to Carthage in 371 for further studies, where his mistress bore him a son, Adeodatus. In 383 he went to Rome and thence to Milan to take a post as professor of rhetoric, adopting the Manichæan religion.

In Milan he met the bishop, St Ambrose, who persuaded him to study the Bible and Christianity, to which he converted in 386. In the same year, he went into retreat with a small group, spending two months in discussion and argument, and writing the first of his philosophical dialogues. In 388 he returned to Tagaste and sold up his father's estate, giving the money to the poor, and, with some friends, lived the monastic life in imitation of the Apostles. On a visit to Hippo, he was ordained a priest to assist the bishop, Valerius. At Hippo he set up a new monastery where all things were held in common and were distributed according to need. He also set himself against various heresies. In 396, the ageing Valerius had Augustine raised to the rank of coadjutor or assistant bishop, and on his death in the same year, Augustine himself became bishop. His episcopal residence now became a monastery for his clerics, but his attempts to persuade higher grades of the ministry to follow suit were largely unsuccessful. Augustine was a prolific writer, but what may have been intended only as a trivial work was a letter to his sister. She was superior of a house of nuns that was apparently in discord. Augustine's letter, written *c* 423, was a set of rules, to be read weekly to the nuns. This letter was the origin of the Rules of St Augustine. Meanwhile, he carried on writing, and finally died at Hippo in 430. In his writings, he left a legacy which was to mould the Christian church for many centuries afterwards.

As a post-script, we can relate that Egelnoth, Archbishop of Canterbury (1020 – 38), while on his way from Rome to Pavia acquired the arm of St Augustine for 100 talents of silver and a talent of gold; he gave it to earl Leofric, and it was housed in a shrine at the Benedictine Priory of Coventry. History does not relate its fate.

THE RULE OF St AUGUSTINE

The full rule is too lengthy to reproduce here, but the following is a condensed version published by Fosbrook[17] in 1817. Although somewhat staccato and quaint, it conveys the application, if not the spirit of the rule, and is derived from that given in *Monasticon*.

RULE 1. Property relinquished by the applicant for admission. Probation by the Prior. Nothing to be taken away by a Canon leaving the order from necessity. Anything offered to be accepted by the Prior's approbation. The rule to be observed from the superior downwards. Punishment denounced for contumacy, and offences to be declared to the Præpositus, before whom disagreements were also to be laid. Property detained through necessity, as above, to be delivered to the Superior.

RULE II. What Psalms, &c. to be sung at the hours and nightly readings immediately after vespers. Labour from morning to Sext, and from Sext to Nones reading. After refection, work till Vespers. Two to be sent together on the Convent business. No one to eat or drink out of the house. Brothers sent to sell things not to do any thing against the Rule. No idle talk or gossiping, but sitting at work in silence.

RULE III. Union in one house. Food and raiment distributed by the Superior. Every thing in common. Consideration to be had of infirmity; against pride on account of difference in birth. Concord. Attention to divine service at the proper hours. Not to make other use of the Church than that it was destined to, except praying in it, out of the proper hours, when they had leisure or inclination. When psalm-singing, to revolve it in the heart. Not to sing but what was enjoined to be sung. Fasting and abstinence. Those who did not fast to take nothing beyond the usual time of dining, except when sick. Reading during dinner. Better food for the sick, not to make the others discontented. Better provisions of clothes for those of delicate habits, not to disgust the others. Sick to be suitably treated during recovery, as suitable; return to the usual habit when well. Habit not conspicuous. To walk together when going out, and stand (stay) together at the journey's end. Nothing offensive in gait, habit or gesture. Not to fix their eyes on women. Mutually to preserve each other's modesty, when two together, in a church where women were. Punishment by the Superior for such offences. Receipt of letters or presents to be punished unless voluntarily confessed. Clothes from one common vestiary, as food from one cellar. Labour for the common good. Vestments sent by relatives to be stored in the common vestiary. Same punishment for concealment as of theft. Clothes washed, according to the order of the Superior either by themselves or fullers. Washing the body in the case of infirmity by medical advice, or, on refusal of that, by order of the Superior.

Not to go to the baths but by two or three, and then with the person appointed by the Superior. Sick to have an infirmarer (fermerer). Cellarers, Chamberlains, or Librarians to serve the brethren with good-will. Books not to be obtained but at the stated hour. Clothes and shoes to be delivered when needed. No lawsuits or quarrels, or terminated as quick as possible. Satisfaction to be made for offences, and speedy forgiveness in the offended. Harsh expressions avoided, and an apology made when uttered. Obedience to the Superior who, if he spoke harsh, was not to beg pardon. Obedience to the head over them, but especially to the Priest (Prior), who had the care of the whole house. Superior, when his authority was not sufficient, to have recourse to that of the Elder or Priest. Superior to govern in charity; to be strict in discipline, yet aim more to be loved than feared. Rule to be read in the presence of the monks (sic) once a week.

6 WARWICKSHIRE DIOCESES

The episcopacy of Warwickshire has undergone considerable change. At the end of the 7th Century, the bishopric of Mercia was divided into two sees. The northern part, the Arden, including Kenilworth, came under the Diocese of Lichfield; the Feldon district, south of the Avon, came in the Bishop of Worcester's diocese. The Warwickshire Augustinian houses of Kenilworth, Arbury and Maxstoke were thus in the Coventry diocese, but Warwick, Studley and Thelsford were in the Worcester diocese, as indeed were some of Kenilworth's appropriated churches.

The Synod of London in 1075 decided that bishops should have their sees in larger towns, and so Bishop Peter moved his seat from Lichfield to Chester, styling himself Bishop of Chester. This transfer was short-lived as the next bishop, Robert de Limesey, who had taken over as Abbot at Coventry, was authorised by the Pope to move the see there in 1102. Although the bishopric was formally that of Coventry, the title of Bishop of Chester continued for some time. Roger de Clinton, Bishop of Coventry (1129-48) and Geoffrey de Clinton I's nephew, is referred to in Kenilworth charters as Bishop of Chester. Roger, incidentally, is claimed by the chronicler, Simeon of Durham, to have bought his see for 3000 marks, perhaps with the assistance of his uncle. In 1228, Lichfield was added to the bishop's title.

Lichfield Cathedral was rebuilt in the 13th Century, and Coventry was largely abandoned by the bishop, except for occasional use of a palace. The title was reversed to Lichfield and Coventry in 1700. In 1886, the archdeaconry of Coventry, comprising the deaneries of Arden, Coventry, Marton and Stoneleigh (including Kenilworth) were transferred to the Diocese of Worcester; but in 1905, the see of Birmingham was created, taking in parts of North Warwickshire, and the archdeaconries of Coventry came under a new see of Coventry, where they remain. Meanwhile, the southern part of the county, which still remained in the Diocese of Worcester, was transferred to Coventry in 1918.

7 WARWICKSHIRE MONASTIC HOUSES

There were more Augustinian houses in Warwickshire than any other order:-

Monasteries

Augustinian Canons:	Arbury, Kenilworth, Maxstoke, Studley, Thelsford and Warwick
Benedictine Monks:	Alcester Abbey, Coventry and Alvecote Priories
Benedictine Nuns:	Polesworth Abbey and Henwood, Nuneaton and Wroxall Priories
Cistercian Monks:	Coombe, Merivale and Stoneleigh Abbeys
Cistercian Nuns:	Pinley Abbey
Carthusian Monks:	St Anne's, Coventry

Friaries

Austin:	Alverstone
Dominican (black):	Warwick
Franciscan (grey):	Coventry
Carmelite (white):	Coventry

There were also the alien Priories of Monks Kirby, Wolston and Warmington, and hospitals and Colleges (such as St Mary, Warwick)

THE OTHER AUGUSTINIAN HOUSES

Arbury

Originally the parish church of Chilvers Coton, Arbury was founded as a priory early in the reign of Henry II by Ralph de Sudley. However, when visited by the Prior of Dunstable under a commission of Pope Gregory IX in 1235, there were only 5 canons there, living a dissolute life. The Pope advised the Bishop of Coventry that the Augustinian Rule should be adopted. When dissolved in 1536, it had a prior, 5 canons and a novice, 9 yeomen, 5 hinds, 2 dairy-maids, 2 corrodians, 6 impotent (helpless) persons with children and 2 persons having fees extraordinary. Its value was £100 5s 5¼d. The pension of the Prior was £13 6s 8d (20 marks). No evidence of the Priory remains.

Maxstoke

A later foundation: Sir William de Clinton, who became Earl of Huntingdon, created a chantry or college of priests at the church of Maxstoke in 1336, when he founded the castle there. It was founded for a prior and 12 canons, and fortunately details of its foundation charter have been recorded. With a value of £112 9s 4¾d, it was dissolved in 1536 with a prior, 5 canons, a novice and 26 dependants: 2 priests to serve the church of Maxstoke and Bentley, 9 yeomen servants, 12 hinds and 3 women servants. The pension of the Prior was £16 6s 8d (20 marks).

The remains of the Priory stand in private grounds, on the south-west-facing slope above a brook that runs into the River Blythe. The standing remains comprise two gatehouses, the crossing tower of the church and the west wall of the Fermery. The inner gatehouse has been incorporated into an Elizabethan house, but the outer gatehouse, adjacent to the road, can be visited by previous arrangement. It is substantially complete, but without a roof. The opening has two bays with a main door and a pedestrian door – as Kenilworth. An octagonal turret, entered from the Priory side, leads to a chamber over the the entrance, which includes a fireplace and chimney, suggesting a room for entertaining. A fine Norman font in Stoneleigh church is said to come from Maxstoke Priory, but it must have had an earlier provenance still.

Studley

Founded by Peter de Corbizon (later de Studley), at Wicton (or Wilton) in Worcestershire, he moved it to Studley early in the reign of Henry II, granting it not only churches, houses and lands, but also a salt furnace at Wiche (Droitwich) and tithes of all his salt. The house lies on flat land east of the River Arrow. The house soon became mismanaged and was down to only 3 canons. Under new patronage of William de Cantilupe, Bishop of Worcester (1237-66), it recovered and flourished and when dissolved it had a prior and 8 canons, and 31 dependants, 6 yeomen, 20 hinds, 4 dairy women and a corrodian. It had a value of £141 4s 9½d. The pension of the Prior was £15. The few remains of the Priory form part of Priory Farm. The nearby Castle, adjacent to the church, was built after the Priory was founded, by a descendant of Peter de Corbizon.

Thelsford

Thelsford has only a marginal claim as an Augustinian house. It, like Warwick, was founded as a house of the Order of the Holy Sepulchre, which followed the Augustinian rule. Founded late in the 12th century, it was dedicated to God, St John and St Radegund. On the fall of Jerusalem it, like all other Holy Sepulchre houses except Warwick, became a Friary of the Order of the Holy Trinity for the Redemption of Captives. The site of the Priory was excavated in advance of the Warwick by-pass in the 1960s by Margaret Grey and is to be reported shortly. There is no building above ground.

Warwick

Henry de Newburgh, the first Earl of Warwick, erected a priory c 1119 on the site of a previous church. He had apparently been asked that it should imitate the independent Augustinian canons of the church of the Holy Sepulchre in Jerusalem. However, on the fall of Jerusalem in 1188 it continued as an Augustinian house under the patronage of the Earl of Warwick. It was valued at £42 7s 4½d in 1536, having a prior and 4 canons when it was dissolved. The pension of the Prior was £5. There are no monastic remains of the Priory, the Warwick County Record Office now occupying the site. The canons' fish-ponds survived until 1851 when some were filled in during the construction of the railway; the rest survived until as late as 1965 before being filled in to make way for an extension to St Nicholas' Park.

KENILWORTH CONVENT'S WHO'S WHO

Superiors & Canons of Kenilworth

in Approximate Chronological Order with an Index

ALPHABETIC INDEX OF NAMES

Philip 1232
POMFRET, Will 1446

QUENTON, Henry de 1351

Ralph 1153
Ralph 1180
Reynold, 1227
Richard 1203
Richard 1227
Richard 1246/7
RIVERS, John 1538
Robert 1298
ROCKESTER, Thomas 1273 1290
Roger 1162
ROGERS, John 1496 1518 1538
ROGERS, Richard 1518
ROLSTON, Henry 1496
RUTH, Henry 1518
RYDEL, George 1538

SALFORD, Roger de 1273 1290
SALLE, Robert de 1292 1312
SALVE, Robert de 1160 1173
SAVAGE, Thomas 1447
SCHREVENHAM, Thomas 1344
SAKERSTON, Robert de 1340
SHAWE, Robert 1462
SHELDON, William de 1309
SHROVESBURY, William 1407
SLOUTH, Adam 1236/7
SMYTHE, Nicholas 1496
SOUTHAM, John 1416
Stephen 1227
Stephen 1310
STOKES, Robert de 1266

STONE, Roger 1426
STONE, Thomas 1518 1538
STONELEY, Thomas 1521
STRECH, John 1407
SUTTON, Rad 1538
Sylvester 1200

TODDE, Richard 1538
TOMWURTHE, Robert 1362
TOWCESTER, Ralph de 1366
TYLLY, Richard 1518
TYNELESFORD, Richard 1279

UNWINE, William 1486

WALLE, William 1516 1518
WALSSHE, Henry 1361
Walter 1204
WALTER, Philip 1496
WANTON, John de 1236/7
WAREWICK, Richard 1496
WARMINGTON, Thomas de 1312 1315 1345
WARWICK, William 1538
WESTON, Henry 1407
WESTON, Robert de 1273 1292
WESTON, William 1423
WHITEWELL, Geoffrey de 1318
WHYTECHURCH, John de 1346
WIGORNIA (Worcester), Roger de 1258 1260
William 1173
WOOTTON, John de 1243
WYCH, John 1369
WYCOMBE, William de 1297
WYRLEY, Will 1455

YARDLEY, Radulphus 1518

ABBOTS, PRIORS & CANONS

(Including those priors of Brooke, Stone and Calwich who would have been
appointed from Kenilworth)

The dates are those of the event first quoted in the text.
Names are of Canons of Kenilworth except where stated.

1124   **Bernard, PRIOR**: he was mentioned as prior in versions of Henry I's foundation charter, and is generally accepted as the first prior. Knowles[23] lists him as prior in 1132, 1139, 1147 and 1148. His possible background is of interest.

A community of Colchester priests seeking a rule sent one of their number, Norman, and his brother, Bernard, to France to study Augustinian practices. They returned to Colchester c 1104, where the Rule was adopted. Norman moved from Colchester to colonise the house of Holy Trinity at Aldgate in London in 1108, where he became the first prior. Geoffrey de Clinton's foundation charter for Kenilworth was witnessed by Norman, Prior of London, and Bernard his brother (Geoffrey had associations with Holy Trinity). There is no doubt that these witnesses were the same pair that went to France; the question is whether the first prior of Kenilworth was that same Bernard. On the face of it, it seems likely, but, according to Watson[44], Bernard was founding Dunstable Priory in 1131-2; if Knowles is right with his last date of 1148, above, Bernard would have been in his late 60s at his last recorded appearance – quite possible.

1135   **Lawrence, PRIOR**: included by Dugdale[14] and *Kenilworth Illustrated*[26] as *temp* Stephen (1135-54), but is not included in the VCH[41]. Watson suggests that he might have been confused with Prior Lawrence of Coventry (1144-79).

1153   **Ralph, PRIOR**: included by Knowles, and mentioned by *Kenilworth Illustrated*, without a date. It is quite possible that he was the Ralph who was Prior of Stone sometime before 1147.

c 1160   **Hugh, PRIOR**: included by Knowles and also Dugdale as Hugo, at the time of Thomas of Canterbury (1162-74), Richard of London (1152-63), Hilary of Chichester (1147-74), John of Worcester (1151-58) and Richard Peche of Coventry (1161-83) (these latter, in fact, under-lap by 4 years).

1154   Baldwin: as a canon of Kenilworth was a witness to a grant by Walter Durdent, Bishop of Coventry, regarding Roger, a canon in the church of St Mary and All Saints, Warwick, having the prebend of the church of Compton Verney

1162   Roger: appears as a Prior of Stone between 1162 and 1178.

1173   Osbert: as a canon of Kenilworth, he witnessed an agreement at Oseney Abbey concerning their church at Bibury; among the other witnesses was a Robert of Kenilworth, presumably the prior, below. Another canon of Kenilworth, William, witnessed a similar agreement, concerning the Abbey's church at Little Rissington.

1160-80   **Robert de SALVE, PRIOR**: given by Kenilworth Illustrated as c 1170 and VCH as 1160-80. He was clearly a man of some legal standing, as he appears, for instance, in 1175, with Roger, Bishop of Worcester, acting as Papal Judge, and also as one of the judges in a dispute between Reading and Gloucester Abbeys. A Papal charter of 1188, confirming the Priory's possessions is addressed to him. As Prior of Kenilworth, he was seen frequently at the Augustinian Abbey of Oseney witnessing charters, receiving statements and making judgements.

1180   Ralph: as prior of the canons' cell at Brooke, he would previously have been a serving canon at Kenilworth.

1200   Hugo de BURGO: appointed by Bishop Mauger of Worcester to a part of the church of Brailes, after Kenilworth had presumably exerted its right of nomination and presentation to the bishop. It is one of the rare cases where a canon is seen to be appointed to a parish church.

1200   Henry: he appears at about this time as Keeper of the Canon's cell at Calwich, appointments being made by Kenilworth canons.

1200/1   **Sylvester, PRIOR**: Dugdale gives him as 2 John (2nd year of King John's reign, namely 18 May, 1200 to 2 May 1201, an unusual span because John's year starts on a moveable feast, Ascension Day)). He was called to the King's Court at Westminster to make a claim for the half knight's fees for Mollington, a part of which village the canons owned. He was probably the same Sylvester who was prior of the canons' cell at Stone 1194-96.

1203   Richard: he appears as Prior of Stone before 1193, and in 1203.

1204   **Walter, PRIOR**: Knowles states that Walter was rightful prior until 1216/17, and that in 1206 there was an intruder, Prior William, who was deposed in 1208. On the other hand, the Annals of Dunstable state that Prior Walter was deposed in 1208 *for his many excesses*. The names appear to have become muddled, and as William de Barton (below) was appointed in 1214, it is assumed that Walter was prior 1204-8. This was followed by a vacancy during the Interdict, when King John handed the Priory over to Henry de Cerne until William de Barton was appointed in 1214, as discussed in Chapter III. Whether Walter was justly deposed might be questioned, as King John may have wished to purloin the revenues of the Priory, which he was entitled to do in the event of the priorship becoming vacant. In 1206, Pope Innocent issued a Bull appointing Walter one of the Judge delegates, with the Abbots of Stoneleigh and Cumbria, to hear a suit involving Luffield Priory.

1214 **William de BARTON, PRIOR:** after the interdict, William de Barton, sub-prior of the Augustinian Abbey of Oseney, Oxford, was appointed prior of Kenilworth. By now, the Priory was certainly under royal patronage.

1221/2 Geoffrey: 'Brother Geoffrey of Kenilworth' acted as the attorney to the Master of the Templars in England in an action against the Earl of Warwick.

1227 Richard, Osbert and Stephen: the King gave the Sub-prior and Convent licence to elect a prior from among these canons. In the event, Henry, below, was elected. Richard might be the same Brother Richard who, in 1246, represented Prior David in a suit as his attorney, but then Richard was a very popular name.

1227 Reynold: appears as Prior of Stone.

1227 **Henry, PRIOR:** previously sub-prior; Henry III approved his election whilst at Windsor on 11 September. During his priorship, he was involved in many property suits at court.

1230 Richard de LICHFIELD: appointed Prior of the canons' cell at Brooke.

1232 Philip: appears as witness in a charter of the Abbey of St Peter, Shrewsbury.

1234/5 Richard de LUDINGTON: One of the canons of Kenilworth, he was presented by Prior Henry to the Bishop of Lincoln as prior of the cell at Brooke. The Bishop invested him and handed him the 'Book of the Priory', possibly a chronicle.

1236/7 Osbert de COVINTRE, Adam SLOUTH and John de WANTON: they brought letters to the King from the Prior and Convent announcing the resignation of the prior and sought licence to elect. No doubt this is the same Osbert as in 1227, above.

1238/9 **David, PRIOR:** all main sources agree 23H3 (1238/39) except the VCH which gives 1236. He had been a Kenilworth canon before his election.

1241 Gilbert: had been Prior of Stone. He was elected Abbot of the Augustinian house of Haughmond, in Shropshire.

1243 John de WOOTTON appointed Prior of Brooke on the death of Richard de LICHFIELD.

1246/7 Richard: 'Brother Richard of Kenilworth' represented David, Prior of Kenilworth, in an action concerning land at Tysoe. [It is unlikely that he was Richard of Ludington or Richard of Lichfield, both of whom had been priors by this time.]

1251 Robert de LEDBURY: appointed to the canons' cell at Brooke, retiring in 1285 and succeeded by Nicholas de BREEDON (see 1276)

1258 John de BRELES, Robert de NENA and Roger de WIGORNIA: they went to the King with letters from the Chapter requesting licence to elect a prior upon the resignation of Prior David.

1258 **Nicholas, PRIOR:** mentioned only by VCH, from Patent Rolls. Nicholas was Prior of Calwich, and was one of the candidates nominated by Henry III, including Robert, Prior of Brooke. During his office, on payment of 26s 4d, he acquired 7 acres of cleared woodland in the Forest of Fakenham, Worcestershire.

1260 WORCESTER, Roger de: appears as Prior of Stone in 1260 and in 1280.

1266 **Humphrey, PRIOR:** again, only the VCH gives his appointment. Royal assent was given for Humphrey, the Cellarer to become Prior. He was only in office for a short while, but was probably prior during the great siege of Kenilworth Castle. He is likely to have been the Humphrey who was Prior of Stone in 1246, when the Priory provided the king with hospitality and provisions.

1266 Robert de STOKES: following a vacancy, licence was given by the King to elect a prior from Robert de Stokes and William de Evesham. In fact Robert de Estleye was elected, with confirmation from the Papal Legate. William de Evesham later became prior, (see 1276 below)

1266/7 **Robert de ESTLEYE, PRIOR:** quoted in all main sources. The Oxford VCH spells it 'Efteley' and relates it to 'Iffley', a church of the Kenilworth canons, just south of Oxford. He resigned 1276. Prior Robert, accompanied by the Abbot of Alcester, had to go to Warwick in 1271 to ban a tournament there in the King's name; he was required to go again in 1272 and 1274 for the same purpose.

1273 Roger de MARLOW and Richard de BRUMSGRAVE: when the King acknowledged that Prior Robert de Estleye was "going beyond the sea", he gave power of attorney to these canons (why was it not given to the Sub-prior?). Richard de Brumsgrove was given dispensation from the Pope in 1290 so that he could minister in the order and accept any office, despite his illegitimate birth, together with Thomas Rockester and Roger de Salford. In 1292, with Robert de Weston, he brought to the King the news of the death of the prior. He became Prior of Brooke between 1294 and 1299, and was, rather surprisingly, not ordained a priest until 1299.

1276   William de MACHEIE: with William de Evesham (see 1266 above), he brought letters from the Chapter to the King, informing him of the resignation of Prior Robert de Estleye.

1276   **William de EVESHAM, PRIOR:** Royal assent was given to his election in March. He died in late 1278 or early 1279 because in February 1279, Edward I appointed vicars to the canons' churches of Chesterton and Lillington, his right as Patron when there was no prior.

1276   Nicholas de BREDON, Sacristan: he was involved in the sad tale of William le Hare who fell to his death from some new work near the church whilst catching wood pigeons, a story which has been brought to life by Irene Potter[29]. His body was found and hidden by the builders, in case the sacristan thought they had killed him. Eventually they and Nicholas de Bredon were imprisoned pending charges, but were finally released when the inquest found it was accidental death. He served as Prior of Brooke between 1285 and 1294, before his retirement.

1279   **Richard TYNELESFORD, PRIOR:** VCH gives him as prior, 1279-92. On February 18, 1288, with the Abbot of Cirencester, he presided over General Chapter of the Order of St Augustine at Dunstable, to which attendance was mandatory. He appears to have made little impression, however, as he *ordained nothing, only enjoyning that the ancient rules be observed.* It may have been in his priorship that St Nicholas' church was consecrated, the first mention of it being in the *1291 Taxio* of Pope Nicholas. The Patron of St Nicholas' was the Prior and Convent of Kenilworth, and continued as such until the Dissolution. It was also in his time that the Pope granted an indulgence to penitents visiting the church of the Priory on the feasts of the Blessed Virgin and St Augustine. In 1290 the Pope also ordered the Bishop of Coventry & Lichfield, following Richard's complaint, not to bring seculars with him into the precinct when he visited, and only two or three of his canons in fitting habit.

1288   Hugo de BROK: a canon of Kenilworth, he was appointed Prior of the Augustinian house of St Sepulchre, Warwick, but was *absolved from the care entrusted to him* by the Bishop on a visitation in July 1293. He died in 1325 and presumably originated from the canons' cell at Brooke.

1290   Thomas ROCKESTER and Roger de SALFORD: with Richard de Brumsgrave, (*see* 1273 above), they were given dispensation for their illegitimate birth. There must have been a purge on the matter of illegitimacy because Richard de Brumsgrave had been given considerable responsibility in the past.

1292   Robert de WESTON: with Richard de Bremesgrave (*sic*), see 1273 above, he brought news of Prior Richard's death to the king.

1292   **Robert de SALLE, PRIOR:** he died in 1312/3.

1297   21st September: At an Ordination by the Bishop of Lincoln at St Mary de Pratis Abbey, Leicester, William de Wycombe *(Wycumbe)* was ordained deacon. At the same ceremony, William of Billesley *(Byllesleye)*, Nicholas de Blagreve, and Henry de Beyville were ordained priests. All came from Kenilworth Priory. The priests had letters dimissory from the Bishop of Coventry and Lichfield [but not the deacon, although other deacons had such letters]. The Examiner for deacons was Master Robert of Kilworth, and for priests, Master Jocelyn, Archdeacon of Stowe. *(The Rolls and Register of Bishop Oliver Sutton of Lincoln, 1280–99, Vol VII, The Lincoln Record Society, Vol 69, 1975)*

1298   Robert: as a Canon of Kenilworth, is listed as a vicar of Ellastone in Staffordshire, which was one of the canons' churches, only 1 km from the canons' cell at Calwich. He is the only canon so listed.

1300   Hugo de KENILWORTH: appointed to the canons' church at Brailes. Could he have been a canon from Kenilworth?

1300   John de FLORE: appointed Prior of Brooke, retiring in 1302, being replaced by Stephen de KETTON.

1305   Richard de BROCK: appointed Abbot of Haughmond, Shropshire, an Augustinian house. He died in 1325, and may also have originated from the cell at Brooke.

1305   John de LEYCESTRE: a canon, he delivered a roll of taxation to the Exchequer. He was keeper of Calwich in 1311 for a short period, being replaced in March, 1312, by John de KETEN for a month only, and then resuming office in May, 1312, possibly until 1318.

1308   Thomas de HOCKLEYE: A Doctor of Divinity, Thomas was ordained priest by the Bishop of Llandaff, the suffragan bishop of Worcester, at Cirencester in 1309, together with 210 acolytes, 89 sub-deacons, 66 deacons and 61 other priests. As he was ordained outside his diocese, dispensation from the Bishop of Coventry and Lichfield was needed. His sepulchral slab was found in the south chapel of the south transept of the church. The following was inscribed in Lombardic brass lettering:

+ ORATE:PRO:ANIME:FRATRIS: THOME:DE:HOCKELE:CUJUS:ANIME PROPICIETUR:DEUS

His brother Robert became Abbot of Stoneleigh and died in 1349, probably of the Black Death.

1309 William de SHELDON: appointed Keeper of Calwich.

1310 Bartholomew de COVENTRY and Thomas BRADWAY: they were sent to the Augustinian Priory at Torksey, in Lincolnshire, where Stephen, the Prior of Brooke, presumably also sent there, had upset the Prior by complaining about him to the Archbishop of Canterbury. Stephen was dragged from the high altar at Torksey, and was imprisoned with the two canons, and was forced to confess that he had betrayed the Prior. After suffering privations, the two canons escaped, and told all to the Pope, who ordered that Stephen, *if still alive*, be released and all be admitted to another house of the order.

1310 Robert de PERSHORE: appointed Prior of Brooke, and may have remained until 1346.

1312 Thomas de BOELES, Precentor: with Thomas de Warmington, below, he brought news to the King of the death of Robert de Salle

1312 Richard de KETEN: appointed Keeper of Calwich, but was only in office for one month, his predecessor, John de LEYCESTRE, taking over again (*see* 1305,) He had been Prior of Brooke in 1299, retiring from there in 1300, but appearing there again as Prior in 1305, until 1310.

1312 **Thomas de WARMINGTON, PRIOR** (previously the Almoner): the Bishop of Coventry & Lichfield received papal confirmation of his appointment. John Rous later wrote of him *Sir Thomas Warmington, prior thereof, Killyngworth, for who God showed oft grate myracles.* During his office, Thomas, Earl of Lancaster, had a chapel built in the castle, to be served by thirteen secular canons. Whatever the motive, and it has been suggested that the Earl had fallen out with the Priory, it did not reach fruition as Earl Thomas was beheaded for treason.

In 1330, the Prior and convent were granted a special dispensation by Edward III, such that when the Priory was vacant, instead of the King claiming the 'temporalities', they were held by the sub-prior and convent. This was to compensate the Priory for the frequent hospitality given to him and his father, Edward II. His tomb, according to Draper [13], was found in the eastern half of the nave and his anniversary was celebrated annually by the canons up to the Dissolution. Carey-Hill quotes Whitley, but without source, as stating that Prior Thomas was a great builder at the Priory.

1315 Will CHARLTON (PRIOR?): he is included in Kenilworth Illustrated only, as prior in 1315/6 (9E2). He was almost certainly not prior as Thomas de Warmington continued until 1345. He might, perhaps, have been sub-prior and he may have come from Charlton Hawthorne in Somerset, where the canons had a church. Alternatively, there may be confusion with Walter Charlton (*see* 1375)

1318 Geoffrey de WHITEWELL: appointed Keeper of Calwich.

1323 Nicholas de BLAGREVE: appointed Keeper of Calwich.

1333 William de BOYDEN: a Keeper of Calwich, (*see* Chapter X), a warrant was made out in 1336 for his arrest if found in the counties of Staffordshire and Derbyshire. He had become *apostate and a vagabond, and is to be returned to Kenilworth to be chastised in accordance with the discipline of his order.* It is not known whether he was caught.

1337 Thomas de HELYDEN: appointed Keeper of Calwich.

1340 Robert de SAKERSTON: appointed Keeper of Calwich.

1344 John LYDZATE and Thomas le SCHREVENHAM: both ordained subdeacons in May 1344 and priests in September, 1345, both by Wolstan de Branford, Bishop of Worcester in Campden Parish church. There are a few instances of the canons being ordained outside their diocese.

1345 Roger de BERMYNGHAM and Stephen de HAVERSHAM: they brought to the King news of the death of Prior Thomas de Warmington and received licence to elect a successor. It is almost certainly the same Roger de Burmingham who became Keeper of Calwich just for the month of August 1349; in 1351, a Roger de Burmingham was appointed vicar of St Nicholas', Kenilworth, having been vicar of Charlton in Somerset, one of the Priory's churches. He was replaced at St Nicholas' probably before 1353, and may have been one of the plague victims.

1345 **John de PEYTO, PRIOR:** Royal assent was given for his appointment. He was ordered by the bishop to have the convent assembled on 21 June, 1361 by order of the king, as the state of the priory had become notorious. What happened on 21 June is not known, and may never be, but he died before 8 August of that year. 1361 saw the re-appearance of the plague, the *Secunda Pestilentia.* Although Bishop Robert de Stretton, of Coventry & Lichfield, wrote in July of 1361 that the *pestilence that God is visiting on the sins of the people, is not yet come into this diocese,* its effect was being noticed in the larger number of appointments to livings by August, peaking in September. Some time would have elapsed after deaths or resignations of the previous incumbent whilst choosing and presenting a new one, so John de Peyto may well have been struck by the plague. It is not clear where he fitted into the famous Warwickshire family of Peyto. Another John de Peyto gave the canons the church and a large part of the village of Loxley in 1350 and died in 1373.

1346	Ordained by Wolstan de Bransford, Bishop of Worcester at Stowe parish church in September: Roger de HYNHAM and John de WHYTECHURCH, acolytes; William de MERSTON and Walter de CHERLTON (*see* also 1375), sub-deacons; Hugh de BOELE, priest.
1346	Geoffrey de HAMPTON: appointed Keeper of Calwich.
1350	Richard de BURGO: granted an *Indult* (a special licence by the Pope) to choose a confessor, who could, at the hour of death, give a plenary remission for all sins 'with the usual safeguards'. This, of course, was the time of the first outbreak of the Black Death, and the giving of indults was to continue until at least 1423.
1351	Henry de QUENTON: ordained a deacon in May 1344 and priest in September 1345, he had now left the order, but wished to return. As a result, Pope Clement VI ordered an inquiry into apostates. This was after the Black Death when the shortage of priests caused some of the rules to be relaxed.
1361	Henry WALSSHE (WALEYS), SUB-PRIOR: he informed the Bishop that John de Peyto had died. He became Prior of Brooke in 1346, and the next recorded appointment there being in 1362.
1361	**Henry de BRADWEYE, PRIOR:** on the death of John de Peyto, licence was obtained from King Edward to choose a replacement. The canons chose Henry de Bradweye, but Bishop Robert de Stretton, of Coventry & Lichfield, ordered a commission to hold an enquiry into the election, and if justice required it, to quash the election, punish the electors and to provide a suitable alternative. However, the commissioners declared the election valid, and the King, as 'Patron and Founder', was duly informed by the Bishop. This enquiry was probably a direct follow-on from the alleged notorious state of the Priory in John de Peyto's time (*see* 1345), when it might have been feared that Henry had been voted in by the canons to perpetuate this unsatisfactory state. The Rule of St Benedict allows bishops to replace abbots found to have been elected to connive at the wickedness of the brethren.
	Henry de Bradweye, almost certainly the same, had been appointed as Keeper of Calwich in 1349 (probably the last before it obtained its independence from Kenilworth),after Roger de Bermyngham, above, and a Henry Bradwas [*sic*] appointed to Haseley church (one of Warwick St Sepulchre's) 15 July, 1325.
	Henry de Bradweye was prior when the Bishop of Coventry, in 1362, on instruction from the Archbishops of Canterbury and York, laid a tax of one tenth on all the goods and benefices of ecclesiastical men, to be paid to the Prior of Kenilworth. This tax was

to raise 100,000 florins which the archbishops, of their own free will, had granted the pope, and which the Pope graciously accepted.

1362	Richard de OXENDON: appointed prior of Brooke, retiring in 1366.

——————— † ———————

At Ordinations by the Bishop of Coventry & Lichfield, the following Kenilworth canons were ordained as indicated:

1362	Hugh de CODYNTON and Robert TOMWURTHE: ordained sub-deacons in March, and became deacons in April 1362 John MARTELL: ordained sub-deacon: James de COLLESHULL became Sub-deacon, and was ordained a priest in 1364, becoming Prior of Brooke in 1388, possibly until 1400.
	William de PEBWORTH and Thomas FARNECOTE: ordained sub-deacons. Thomas Farncote become Prior of Brooke in 1375.
1364	John de COVENTRY: ordained Sub-deacon in October, and Deacon in June 1367. It was probably the same John de Coventry who, in 1389, was pardoned at the intervention of Prior Thomas Merston for having stolen goods and chattels belonging to the Prior, and taking money from William Dexter who was residing in the Priory. A monk of Stoneleigh, John de Coventre, became abbot there in 1401, but is unlikely to be the same person.
1366	Ralph de TOWCESTER: appointed Prior of Brooke, retiring in 1375.
1369	James HASELHOLT: ordained deacon, and priest in 1372.
	John AVERY and John WYCH: ordained deacon, and became priests in the same year.
	Thomas LICHFIELD and Henry ALDERMARSTON: ordained deacons
1376	Thomas BOHFELD: ordained deacon
1377	Thomas DALAM: ordained sub-deacon

——————— † ———————

1375	Walter de CHERLTON, PRIOR: given in VCH only. In an exchange of vicars between Sandford St Martin in Lincolnshire, and Salford Priors in 1381, there is a reference to 'Bro Walter, Prior and Convent of Kenilworth'. The Will Charlton of 1315 of *Kenilworth Illustrated* may have been confused with him.
1379	Robert of LEICESTER: appointed Prior of Brooke, retiring in 1385.
1385	**Thomas MERSTON, PRIOR:** all sources agree. He was ordained sub-deacon in 1362, and priest in January 1364.
1400	**Walter BRAYLIS, PRIOR:** all sources agree. He resigned 1403
1400	Henry BLACKWELLE: He had the dignity of Papal Chaplain conferred upon him.

1400   Thomas CAMPDEN: appointed Prior of Brooke.

1403   **Thomas KIDDERMINSTER, PRIOR**: John Burghill, Bishop of Coventry and Lichfield, signified the Royal assent to his election. He was ordained sub-deacon in 1375 and priest in 1377. There was a problem with his sub-diaconate because his ordination was carried out by one William who pretended to be the rightful Bishop Bellenen; it could not be proved that this William had the necessary powers, so Thomas and others, including Henry de Aldermarston, had to be ordained again. He became Prior of Brooke in 1385, retiring back to Kenilworth in 1388. His name was given to the Great Bell which was recast in 1734, and again in 1875. It had been granted to the parish church on Dissolution, and bore the inscription **T KEDERMYNSTRE P. DE K. MENTEM SANTATAM SPONTONEUM HONOREM DEO, PATRIE LIBERATIONEM ANGELUM PACIS MICHAEL AD ISTRAM CELITUS MITTI ROGITAMUS AULAM.**

1403   Richard CHARLTON: appointed Prior of Brooke, retiring in 1407.

1407   Henry WESTON and William SHROVES-BURY: canons OSA (Order of St Augustine) of Kenilworth, were ordained priests at Blockley in the Diocese of Worcester, for which there was a Dimissory Letter allowing them to be ordained outside their diocese. William (Shrewsbury) appointed Prior of Brooke in 1425.

1407   John STRECH: appointed Prior of Brooke, retiring in 1425.

1416   John SOUTHAM: ordained a deacon by Simon Brampton at Coventry in September 1416. In May, 1418, he is also recorded as being ordained at Lichfield by the Bishop of Killaloe, again as a deacon, (the reason for this is not clear). The bishop would have been the suffragan, or assistant, bishop, as suffragans' titles were taken from remote Irish or Mediterranean towns (Killaloe is near Limerick, Southern Ireland). He was ordained a priest by the same bishop in June, 1419.

1418   Richard NAPTON: ordained a deacon in May 1418 by Bishop Killaloe, and for some reason, again ordained as deacon in June 1419.

1419   Robert MULFIELD: ordained a priest by Bishop Killaloe in June 1419

1423   William WESTON was granted a Papal Indult to choose his own confessor. (*see* 1350)

1426   Thomas NORTON, SUB-PRIOR: according to the VCH, he was sent by Bishop Heywood to the cell at Brooke for being obstinate and contumacious. However, an unknown annotator of a copy of the VCH claims that this occurred in 1446, and that it was Prior Thomas Holygreve who took this action (*see* Chapter X).

1426   Roger STONE: with Thomas Holygreve, below, he was sent to Stone for leaving the cloister without permission. The unknown annotator (*see* above) has written in the margin that only Roger was sent.

1433   Thomas BLACKWELL: appointed Prior of Brooke, but, for whatever reason, was replaced within a year by Thomas LAYTON, who died in 1453.

1439   **Thomas HOLYGREVE, PRIOR and FIRST ABBOT**: he was elected Prior of Stone in 1423 immediately following the resignation of his predecessor, Ralph of Stamford. In 1439 he was appointed with the Abbot of Leicester, Prior of Southwark, and the Prior of Newark, all Augustinian, to take the Augustinian Priory of Christ Church, London, into their care for 2 years, due to its misrule.

He was appointed visitor of the Diocese of Coventry & Lichfield, and also of St Asaph, North Wales. The latter was not visited, however, *as the people there and the language was almost unknown to the visitor, and there seemed to be no safe way of approach.*

He was elected Prior of Kenilworth on 5 August, 1439, and became the first abbot between 1447 and 1450 (*see* Chapter XI). The report that he was sent to Stone in 1426 for disciplining, as discussed in Chapter X, appears unlikely as he was already prior there by that date.

1446   Will POMFRET: having served as a canon, he became Vicar of Leamington Priors on 10 May 1446, and he resigned not later than in 1455.

1447   **Thomas SAVAGE, PRIOR**: the only evidence for his being prior, or indeed associated with Kenilworth, is from *Kenilworth Illustrated*, and no source is quoted. The question of his existence is discussed in Chapter XI.

1453   Thomas BRAYLES: appointed Prior of Brooke, retiring in 1459.

1455   Will WYRLEY, PRIOR: *Kenilworth Illustrated* is again alone in listing him; there was by now also an Abbot.

1458   **John ERDELEY, ABBOT**: also known as Yardley, main sources agree he became Abbot 2 May, 1458. In the following year, out of *special grace to John Yardley, the Abbot, with his successors* in Kenilworth, was granted special rights in its manors – see Chapter VIII.

1459   Richard MARSTON: appointed Prior of Brooke, retiring in 1519.

1462   Robert SHAWE: a professed canon, is granted Papal dispensation to receive any benefice and act as a secular priest, thus releasing him from his professional vows. He has not been identified as serving at any of the canons' churches.

1486 William UNWINE: succeeds Richard MERSTON as Prior of Brooke, both having served at Kenilworth.

1494 **Ralph MAXFIELD, ABBOT**: main sources agree 11 January, 1494. He constructed the deer park at Rudfyn.

———— † † ————

The following were at the Abbey at Bishop Blythe's Visitation, as well as Abbot Ralph Maxfield:

1496 John BALSALE, Sacrist; Robert BROMEALL, Cellarer; Richard COLSHILL, Almoner; William CURTLYNTON, Sub-prior; Hugh GLEVE, professed canon; John HASEBERRY, professed canon; Robert HERVEY, novice; John LYSTER, novice (see also 1534); Thomas MOGGE, Prior; John ROGERS, professed canon (see also 1538); Henry ROLSTON, Kitchener; Nicholas SMYTHE, novice [and by 1506 he was a canon and one of the four leaders of a procession at the Chapter of the Order at Barnwell]; Philip WALTER, Precentor; Richard WAREWICK, professed canon.

———— † † ————

1516 **William WALLE, ABBOT**: main sources all agree this date. In 1494, a William Wall Pbr (presbyter or priest) was at Stoneleigh church. William Wall of Kenilworth appeared in 1509 at the Chapter of the Order at Leicester, where he gave the first sermon. In 1523 he was given the civil honour of being on the Commission of Peace for Warwickshire, the only religious superior in the Shire to have this honour, this commission being renewed in 1529, 32 and 34. In 1533 he had to preside over an important enquiry with the mayor of Coventry and two county justices. In his letter to Cromwell of June 1536 regarding Brooke (*see* Chapter X), he mentions the service that he gave to the King during the insurrection in Coventry. There were two plots to take Kenilworth Castle, in 1523 and 1524, but in both cases the plotters were hanged, drawn and quartered. Could he have provided a service here?

It was probably William Walle who went hunting with Sir Henry Willoughby, Knight of the Holy Sepulchre and Commissioner of Warwickshire, who had his house at Middleton and died in 1528/9.

———— † † † ————

The following are named as present at Bishop Geoffrey Blythe's visits in 1518, 1521 and 1524. Their presence and rôles outside the dates given must be assumed unless otherwise stated.

1518 Robert ALCESTRE: Fermery Master 1518-24.

Hugo BOLTON: Almoner 1518-24.

Edmund BONDE: Fraterer, but by 1521 was Kitchener and continued until at least 1524.

Thomas COVENTRY: Novice, by 1521 he was Succentor, and Precentor by 1524.

William LEYCESTRE: Novice, by 1521 he was Fraterer but was no longer listed for 1524.

John LICHFIELD: Abbot's Chaplain 1518-24.

John LYSTER: *See* 1534.

Robert ORWELL: Prior: 1518-24, then appearing as Prior of Brooke in 1531, and dying in 1534.

John PENKETH: Cellarer, listed for 1518 only; he became Prior of Brooke in 1519, retiring from there in 1525.

John ROGERS: he appears 1518-24 and also 1538/9 (*q.v.*), always as a canon.

Richard ROGERS: Treasurer and Kitchener, he was Cellarer by 1521, until at least 1524, and was Prior of Brooke in 1525, retiring in 1531.

Henry RUTH: at the visitations of 1518 and 1521 he was ill, the second time with gout, and was unable to attend; he was not listed for the 1524 Visitation (a Henry Ruth, Chaplain, was appointed to Honiley church on 20 January, 1495.

Richard TYLLY: Sacrist, 1518-24.

Thomas STONE: a Novice in 1518 and 1521, but Master of the Novices by 1524; see also 1538/9.

William WALLE: ABBOT, *see* 1516.

Ralph YARDLEY: a Novice, 1518-24.

1521 Roger HARWELL: a Novice 1521-24, he became Prior of Brooke in 1534, and was the last prior there.

Simon JEKYS: *See* 1537.

Thomas STONELEY: a novice 1521-24.

———— † † † ————

1534 **John LYSTER, PRIOR**: He appears in 1496 as a novice, was listed as sub-prior 1518-24, and became a member of the Corpus Christi Guild of Coventry. This Guild, with the Trinity Guild, dominated the Coventry Corporation. Membership of one of these was probably necessary to obtain an office in the town. At the Dissolution, he received a pension of £8.

1537 **Simon JEKYS, ABBOT**: he surrendered the Priory to the King's commissioners on 15 April, 1538. He received a pension of £100 a year, and Dugdale suggests he retired to

Rudfyn. He was listed as a novice in 1521 and 1524.

———— † † † † ————

With Simon Jekys and John Lyster, above, the following were named by Dugdale. He gives two lists of names, the first of the 'convent', names taken to be those present at 15 April, 1538 and the second, names of those pensioned on 6 May, 1539.

These lists are not identical, as seen below:

1538-39

Richard BADGE: Sub-sacrist in 1521, he was one to complain of the severity of the prior and sub-prior, and criticised the quality of the food given to the sick. He even accused the prior and sub-prior of allowing women into their cubicles. He received a pension of £6 at the Dissolution, and is found at Harbury Church in 1550, as priest.

Randolph BAXTER: pension £5. A Randulphus Baxter was appointed in April 1559 to the church at Newnham Regis, of which Kenilworth had had the patronage. A John Baxter served at Newnham from 1534 to his death in 1552.

William CLARE: pension £5. (Any connection with the Austin Friary at Clare, Suffolk, unlikely)

Richard HETHE: pension £5 6s 8d, probably from Hethe, Oxfordshire, where the Abbey had a church.

Richard PALMER: pension £5. A Richard Palmer was appointed in 1564 to the church at Wolvey, which was in the patronage of Lichfield Cathedral. Also, a Richard Palmer served at the church of Stretton Baskerville from 1569 to possibly 1581.

Thomas PARKER: pension £5 6s 8d. A Thomas Parker was appointed in 1542 to Ashow church, serving to possibly 1565. Ashow had been one of the Abbey's churches.

John RIVERS: pension £5. His name is missing from the 'convent' list

John ROGERS: he was a problem, and thus, although a canon for at least 20 years, was never promoted. According to Richard Rogers, probably his brother or cousin, he had been severely punished c 1518, and other canons claimed he brought disrepute to the House. For his part, he criticised the superiors for laughing at him when he brought complaints, and for bringing about injustices. He also criticised the falling standards of the House. At the Dissolution he received the higher pension of £7, and was dispensed from his vows in 1539.

George RYDEL: pension £5 6s 8d

Thomas STONE: pension £7. He was a novice in 1518 and 1521, and was Master of Novices by 1524

Richard TODDE: pension £5. A Richard Todd was a novice at the Augustinian Priory of Maxstoke in 1518, and a Richard Todde was appointed to Claverdon church (not one of Kenilworth's) in 1543 as the priest there.

William WARWICK: pension £6. A William Warwick was appointed to Alveston church on the 19th October, 1549

The following appear on the 'convent' list, but not among those receiving pensions. They were probably novices.

William CHAMBERLAIN
John LUFFKYN
Rad SUTTON

REFERENCES

1 Aston, M *et al*: Warwickshire Fishponds, *Medieval Fish, Fisheries & Fishponds in England*, BAR British Series, 182 (i) 1988

2 Baugh, G C & Cox, D C: *Monastic Shropshire*, Shropshire Libraries, 1982

3 Bickley, W B: *Abstract of the Bailiffs' Accounts of Monastic & Other Estates in the County of Warwick*, Dugdale Society, 1923

4 Carey Hill, E: Kenilworth Abbey, *Transactions of the Birmingham Archæology Society*, Vol LII, OUP 1930

5 Carey Hill, E: *The Abbey of St Mary, Kenilworth*, 1937, Reprinted by the Odibourne Press, 1985

6 Chatwin, Philip B: Medieval Coffin Lids from Longbridge, *Trans Birmingham Archæology Society*, Vol 60, 1940

7 Chatwin, Philip B: Medieval Patterned Tiles of Warwickshire, *Trans Birmingham Archæology Society*, Vol 60 (1940) pp 1–41.

8 Clark, John W, MA FSA: *The Observances in Use at the Augustinian Priory of Barnwell, Cambridge*, Macmillan & Bowes, Cambridge, 1897

9 Cooper, M: Kenilworth Abbey Foundations, *Kenilworth History & Archæology*, September 1977.

10 Cox, David: *The Chronicle of Evesham Abbey*, Evesham Historical Soc, 1964.

11 Deansley, Margaret: *A History of the Medieval Church 590 – 1500*, Methuen, 1947 (revised)

12 Dickinson, Rev J C: *The Origins of the Austin Canons and their Introduction into England*, SPCK, 1950

13 Draper, W H: On St Mary's Abbey, Kenilworth, *Rugby School Natural History Society Report*, 1891

14 Dugdale, Sir William: *The Antiquaries of Warwickshire*, Dr William Thomas' version, 1730.

15 Dugdale, Sir William: *Monasticon Anglicanum*, New Edition, 1846

16 Ellis, Roger H: *Catalogue of Seals in the PRO*, HMSO 1986

17 Fosbrook, Thomas D: *British Monachism or Manner & Customs of the Monks and Nuns of England*, John Nichols, 1817.

18 Greene, J Patrick: The Elevation of Norton Priory, Cheshire, to the Status of a Mitred Abbey, *Trans Historic Society of Lancashire & Cheshire*, Vol 128, 1978.

19 Harvey, John H: Sidelights on Kenilworth Castle, *Royal Archæological Institute of Great Britain and Ireland*, 1946 Vol CL

20 Hilton, R H (Editor): *Stoneleigh Leger Book*, Dugdale Society, OUP, 1960

21 Holliday J R: Communication of 5 April 1876, *Trans Birm Arch Soc* Vol VII,

22 John, Trevor: *The Warwickshire Hundred Rolls of 1279–80, Stoneleigh and Kineton*

23 Knowles, Dom David: *Heads of Religious Houses 940 – 1216*

24 Lamb, Dr R G: *Abbey Gatehouse, Kenilworth 1977*, Warwick County Museum, limited circulation.

25 Lawrence, Prof C H: *Medieval Monasticism*, Longman, 1984

26 Merridew: *Kenilworth Illustrated*, Merridew & Sons *et al*, 1821.

27 Nicklin, Phyllis A: Early Arden, *Trans Birmingham Archæology Society*, 1936

28 Pevsner & Wedgewood: *Warwickshire*, Buildings of England series, Penguin Books, 1966

29 Potter, Irene: *Tales of Old Kenilworth*, Warwick Printing Co, 1985

30 Robinson, David M: *The Geography of Augustinian Settlement in Medieval England & Wales*, BAR British Series 80(i), 1980

31 Salter, Rev H E: *Chapters of the Augustinian Canons*, Oxford Historical Society, Clarendon Press 1922

32 Southern, R W: *Western Society & the Church in the Middle Ages*, Penguin, 1970

33 Stevens, N: The Origins of Kenilworth Castle, *Kenilworth History 1994*, Kenilworth History & Archæology Society.

34 Sunley, Harry: *Kenilworth Chronology*, Odibourne Press, 1989

35 Sunley, Harry: *Medieval Crockford – Warwickshire*, in preparation for limited publication

36 Sunley, Harry: Recent Observations on the West Doorway of St Nicholas' Church, Kenilworth, *Trans Birmingham & Warwickshire Archæological Society* for 1987–8, Vol 95

37 Sunley, Harry: Recent Observations on the Monks' Hole, St Nicholas Churchyard, *Kenilworth History 1993*, Kenilworth History & Archæology Society, 1993

38 Sunley, Harry: Little Virginia, *Account Rendered*, Kenilworth History & Archæology Society, 1983

39 Sunley, Harry: *Kenilworth Abbey Medieval Window Glass*, Kenilworth History & Archæology Society, 1991. Limited circulation including County Museum, Corpus Vitrearum Medii Aevi, Gt Britain.

40 Trevelyan, G: *History of England*, Longmans, 1960

41 Various: *Victoria County History of Warwickshire*, OUP, 1949

42 Walsgrove, Stephen G: *Kenilworth 1086–1756*, Warwick Printing Co, 1991

43 Walsgrove, Stephen G: Aspects of High Street, *Kenilworth History 1992*, Kenilworth History & Archæology Society.

44 Watson C: *The Kenilworth Cartulary*, unpublished, on micro-film, Warwick Records Office; in book form at Institute of Historical Research – limited access.

45 Whitley, T W: *Handy Guide and History of the Ruins of St Mary's Abbey, Kenilworth...*, c 1895.

INDEX

References are to Page and Column, except for four-digit numbers which refer to dates in the 'Who's Who' listing

Papal *(contd)* Judge, Prior as 1160
 Mandate 1290
 Protection of Priory 7 b
Parliament, Prior called to 20 b
Patron, rôle of 7 a
Patronage of Kenilworth Churches 22 b
 royal, effect of 8 b
Pensions, at Dissolution 55 a
Peyto, John, & the Black Death 24 b
 & the notorious state of Priory 1345
Polesworth Nunnery, royal exemption of 52 a
Poor, concern for 19 a
Pope Benedict, constitutions of 5 a
 Gregory IX, charter 7 b
 Honorius II, Bull 7 a
 Innocent III, Interdict 7 b
 Nicholas V, draft letter 50 a
Portchester, Priory in castle 5 b
Porter, John le 27 b
Præmonstratensians 3 a
Presentation of incumbents 18 a
Priests, Celibacy of 1 a
Prior, Bernard, first Prior 6 a 1124
 Holygreve, Thos, rôle in elevation to Abbey 51 a
 John Peyto, 'notorious state of Priory' 52 a
 Silvester, appointment of 7 b
 Thomas Savage, significance of 50 a
 Walter, deposed 7 b
 William Barton, Sub-prior of Oseney 8 a
 William Barton, Tournament ban 19 b
Prior, duties as,
 Clerk of works 20 b
 Commissioner of peace 20 a
 Diocesan visitor 20 a
 Godfather 20 b
 Host 20 a
 Papal commission 20 b
 President of Chapter of Order 20 b 1279
 Receiver of issues 19 b
 Rôle at Stone 48 a
 Tenancies in Warwickshire 27 a
 Travel overseas 1273
 Visitor to S Asaph's 1439
Priories, beside castles 6 a
 time taken to build 6 a
Priorsfield, quarry 5 b
Priory, dedication of 6 b
 fined by General Chapter 10 a
 in king's hands 7 a
 in Pope's protection 7 b
 in secular hands 7 b
 income, compared 24 a
 notorious state of 1345
 Officers of 10 b
 privileges as lord of manor 27 a
 vacancy 7 b 9 a
Processions, canons' 16 a
Punishment 17 b
Pynham Priory, foundation 14 a

Radford Semele, licence in Mortmain 22 b
Rector, difference from vicar 19 a
Royal Foundation & patronage 8 b
Royal visitors 1312
Rudfyn 24b 53b 54a 1494 1537

Ss Anthony & Basil 1 a
S Augustine of Hippo, The Rule 62 b
S Frideswide, Oxford 3 a
S Mary's Priory, Coventry
 purchase of royal exemption 52 a
S Mary's, Warwick, Kenilworth coffin lids 56 b
S Nicholas' Church,
 churchyard encroaching Abbey site 55 b

S Nicholas' Church *(contd)* lightning strike on 55 b
 sedilia 55b
 west door 55 a
S Osyth's Priory 3 a
S Remy, Juliana 23 b
S Ruf, canons 1 b
S Simon Stylites 1 a
School, at Bushmead Priory 18 b
School, canons' 18 b
School Lane Meadow 32 a
Scriptorium 16 a
Seals of Abbey/Priory 8b 62 a
Semilly,
 Geoffrey de Clinton's Castle at 58 a
 William de 58 a
Sickness, canons' 15 b
Siege of Kenilworth 8 b
Silence, rule of 15 a
Spiritualities 22 b
 listed 29 ff
Stephen Langton, election of priors 8 a
Stone, cell of Kenilworth 48 a
 rules of 48 b
Students, requirement to send to university 5 a
Studley Priory, near a castle 5 b
 threatening behaviour 52 a
Superior, rôle of 19 a
Suppression of lesser monasteries 53 a

Tankerville, William de 58 a
Taverns, canons visiting 16 b
Tax collection by superior 20 a
Temporalities, held by king 8 a
 in Kenilworth 23 b
 listed 29 ff
Thomson, Revd Jack 57 a
Tiles, floor 55 a
Tithes, failure to hand over 22 a
 vicarial & rectorial 23 a
Torksey Priory, high adventure at 1310
Tournament ban by Priors 19 b
Tysoe, land granted in 23 b

University, scholars sent to 10 a

Valence, Aymer de, 23 a
Vicar, difference from rector 19 a
Vicarage *viii* a
Visitation, bishop's 8 b
Visitor, Diocesan, Prior as 20 a
Visitors, Diocesan 14 a
Voidance (or vacancy) of Priory 8 a

Walle, Abbot William, & Brooke 49 b
Waltham Cross, foundation of 2 a
Warwick Castle 5 b
Warwick, Earl of, his canon 15 a
Warwickshire Dioceses 63 b
Water supply, Priory's 34 b
Wells, Hugh de, holds Priory 7 b
Weston under Wetherley, licence in Mortmain 22 b
Whitley, T W, excavation by 56 a
Windmill at Harbury 27 b
Window glass, stained and painted 56 a
Wolsey, Cardinal, concern for order 52 b
 death of 3 b
Wolston, licence in Mortmain 22 b
Women, canons' contact with 16 b
Wootton, Godwin de, burial grant 23 b
Worksop, canons as vicars 18 a
Wridfen *(see also Rudfyn)* 26 b
Wycliffe, John of Lutterworth 52 b
Wyse, Thos, Prior of Stone excommunicated 48 b